Numerology & Crystals

Have Unstoppable Success in Your Career, Relationships, Make Your Dreams A Reality and Heal & Empower Your Life with Numerology and Crystal Energy

Written by

Mia rose

Content

Numerology

The Ultimate Guide to uncovering your Future, Creating Success &

Making your Dreams a Reality using the Art & Science of Numbers

Written By

Mia Rose

Introduction

I want to thank you and congratulate you for getting the book, "The Ultimate Guide to Numerology".

This book contains all the information you need to create Numerology Charts for yourself, friends or other people. Explaining how to calculate Personal Numbers, Soul Numbers, Life Path Numbers and Destiny Numbers, along with detailed description of the meaning of each, this book provides both basic information and detailed Numerology descriptions. Looking at single and double digit vibrations the book provides a detailed, comprehensive information allowing you to create complex Numerology profiles.

Thanks again for reading this book, I hope you enjoy it!

Part 1: The Art and Science of Numerology

Numbers are everywhere and rule our lives from the moment we are born. Time, money, weights, measures and even the Universe are all expressed in numbers. The modern symbols that we use to express numbers are simply expressions of concepts, and very powerful ones at that. While it could be argued that numbers are abstract concepts they are, in fact, very real. All life begins as a single cell, dividing and multiplying. The universe itself is understood to have had a single starting point, growing and multiplying through time. Numbers resonate behind all of creation and for many centuries numbers have been regarded as not only the basic 'format' behind creation but powerful forces that impact on our lives and existence at a deeper level.

The Father of Mathematics – and More.

Numerology is the science and art of studying how numbers and their vibrations influence our personality and the paths that our lives take. It has origins in Ancient Greece, when Pythagoras developed the philosophy behind Numerology. Pythagoras is, today, better known as the "Father of Mathematics" but was also, in his own era, a renowned philosopher and a great mystic. Pythagoras' understanding of the Universe was based on the simple fact that numbers were what governed it – a fact that modern science cannot argue with. Everything could be defined in numbers and everything, according to his theories, was profoundly influenced by the vibrations of numbers. Geometry and Astrology were also areas of science that Pythagoras was intrigued by and, again, he found that understanding numbers allowed him to decode their mysteries.

How Numerology Works.

Pythagoras' system of Numerology is the basis of the modern art and science. It is based on the concept that everything in the Universe is governed by cycles and that these cycles can be predicted. The means of interpreting these cycles, that Pythagoras developed, is based on the use of the numbers 1-9. All other numbers above 9 can be reduced to one of these basic figures. For example 12 is comprised of the individual digits 1 and 2, which added together produce 3. In the same way the number 1278 can be reduced to 9 by adding the individual numbers, 1+2+7+8 which totals 18 which is further reduced to 9.

In addition to these main numbers four other numbers are also considered when practicing Numerology. These are; 11, 22, 33 and 44. These are not normally reduced (to 2, 4, 6 and 8) for the purposes of creating an accurate reading. As Master

Numbers they are considered to contain the principles of their base number (that number to which they can be reduced) but to have an independent meaning in their own right and to enhance the significance of the messages contained in Numerology.

Your Personal Numbers.

When we are born we each receive four specific sets of numbers which are significant for the purposes of Numerology. These are defined as follows; the Life Lesson Number, the Soul Number, the Outer Personality Number and the Path of Destiny Number. In this book we will look at all four numbers and how to calculate them. In addition we will look at the meanings traditionally ascribed to the numbers under the Pythagorean system.

This system also uses a double number and single number system. Ultimately, as we have seen, all numbers can be reduced to a figure between 1-9. These are the 'core' principles of the numbers but the initial figures that we come to when we calculate our personal numbers can be expressed as double figures. While these double figures are normally reduced to a single digit they are also useful as they offer a more detailed insight into the way these numbers influence us. These numbers are 1 – 78, with higher numbers reduced accordingly.

What's in a Name?

Numerology uses both birth dates and names for the purpose of calculating the relevant numbers. In the case of names, these should be the full birth name given on your birth certificate. Name changes due to marriage, from choice or the use of shortened/nicknames are not considered to be relevant for numerology purposes. However, some practitioners do argue that you may be influenced by numbers resulting from a name change and it is possible to use them if you wish. However, the original birth name should be used for the basic reading and can be combined as a fuller reading when using a new or altered name. In many cases it's considered that the Destiny Number may be strongly influenced by a change of name and this is one occasion on which it can be useful to use both the birth and any subsequent name when preparing a reading.

How to Calculate Your Personal Numbers.

Each letter of the alphabet is assigned a number, starting at 1 through to 26. A-I are expressed as 1-9, while above this the letters are expressed as double and single digits. For example, P is expressed as 16/7 or W as 23/5. Using this system of numbering is the basic tool for calculating each of the relevant numbers. For reference the table below is useful;

A 1	J 10/1	S 19/1
B 2	K 11/2	T 20/2
C 3	L 12/3	U 21/3
D 4	M 13/4	V 22/4
E 5	N 14/5	W 23/5
F 6	O 15/6	X 24/6
G 7	P 16/7	Y 25/7
H 8	Q 17/8	Z 26/8
I 9	R 18/9	

Note: the Master Numbers in the above table (11 and 22) have been reduced. If they appear in your own calculations, or those done for others, they should be read in their Master format and their reduced format to provide a detailed reading.

Calculating the Life Lesson Number.

The Life Lesson number is calculated from your full birth date and it is the number that rules us from birth. It is most important in our choices of career, as it is in this area of life that we are likely to develop our skills to their full potential. Everything has a birth date, so this number can be used to establish the future prospects of most new ventures in life – be that a job or new business, a move or a marriage. Using the example of a birth date of 21ˢᵗ June 1974 we calculate the Life Lesson as follows;

The date should be used in full and expressed as follows: 06 21 1974 (the US format, although the commonly used European format – 21 06 1974 can also be used). To calculate the birth number first reduce the birth year to a two digit format; so in this case 1+9+7+4 = 21.

Now add the month and date to this number; 6 + 21 + 21 = 48. this number can be reduced to 12 (4 + 8) which is further reduced to 3 (1+2). The resulting number for numerology purposes is expressed as **48/3.**

This is the Life Lesson number for those born on that date. Both numbers (48 and 3) are significant. In the next chapter we look at the definitions for the numbers 1-9 (plus the Master Numbers 11, 22, 33 and 44) in relation to the Life Lesson, the Soul Path, the Outer Personality and the Path of Destiny Numbers. Using that chapter you can use these to establish the meaning of your life lesson number. However, in the example above, 48 is also important as it gives a more detailed definition and outline. This should be used to explore the deeper influence of your Personal Numbers. Each element of the number vibrates in different ways; so although 3 can be arrived at by many numerical combinations, in this case 48 will show how it operates in relation to the relevant personal number. The detailed definitions of these vibrations are listed in the meaning of your life Lesson Number. The detailed definitions for the double digit numbers can be found in Part 3 of the book.

The Soul Number.

This is calculated by using the full name given at birth (see the note on name changes above) and is derived from the vowels* in that name only. In this example we will use the name "Phillip James Hall".

The calculation for this name would be done as follows;

I/9, I/9, A/1, E/5 and A/1.

$9 + 9 + 1 + 5 + 1 = 25/7$.

* The vowels, are A, E, I, O, U; however, for numerology purposes it should be noted that Y is also considered a vowel when no other vowels appear in the syllable (examples being

Sybil or Cyril). In both of these case the "vowels" used to calculate the number would be Y and I.

In the example of Phillip James Hall, above, the Soul Number is calculated as 25/7. The 7 is the significant number, outlining the basic core principles and attributes bestowed on the individual. The Soul Number is about our real selves – it's represents who we truly are and often is only known to ourselves, not to those around us in life. To read the attributes and vibrations bestowed by this number, Matthew would first look at the meaning of the soul number 7 and then for a broader definition at the description of 25/7 in Part 3. This explains how his inner self is influenced and the deeper vibrations of the number 7.

The Soul Number is a strong representation of our deepest desires and is believed to represent what we have learned in past lives. For this reason the soul number can have a profound influence on our needs in this world and on our motivations and ways of achieving what we desire. It is possible for the deeply rooted urges expressed in the Soul Number to overshadow the other numbers and, for this reason, it is the number that you should pay the closest attention to.

The Outer Personality Number.

This number denotes how we appear to the outside world. It is *not* necessarily a good definition of who we truly are but better understood as the way in which we are perceived. If the Soul Number represents who we really are, this number represents how we present ourselves to the outside world. This is significant in that it can affect the way in which people understand us and also in what they will expect from us in life. There can be significant differences in the meanings of the Soul Number and the Outer Personality Number and this can lead to expectations from others that are not realistic – or not that we cannot meet. The Outer Personality Number is calculated using the consonants only from the full birth name. Using the example of Phillip James Hall, as above, we would make the following calculation.

P/7, H/8, L/3, L/3, P/7, J/1, M/4, S/1, H/8, L/3, L/3.

7+8+3+3+7+1+4+1+8+3+3 = 48/3.

In this case the individual would read the description for 3 (48 reduces to 12 which, in turn, is reduced to 3) as his Outer Personality number and, for greater detail, the description of 48/3 as a Personality number, bearing in mind the relevance and meaning of a Soul Number as the real, inner personality that drives your urges in life.

The Personal Destiny Number.

This, the last of your four personal numbers, focuses on what you must achieve in life, the lessons you must learn and forces which will benefit (or cross) you in life. Of the four numbers this is the one which may be altered by name changes; whether through use of shortened or nickname, or through a change of name brought about by marriage or simply through choice. Most Numerologists agree that these changes can influence your life path by altering the vibrations which will affect you. This is significant in that it relates to the way in which our choices in life affect our future and our destiny.

This number can reflect our free will and, for this reason, many numerologists consider it acceptable (advisable even) to read this number based on both the original birth name and any name currently used by the subject. We'll use our example again of Phillip James Hall and in this case we'll look at both his birth name and the name he is commonly known by – "Jim Hall".

Calculating the Destiny number is simple; we use all the letters of the name (effectively adding the Soul and Outer Personality Numbers together). In Jim's case we'll demonstrate the calculation by looking at his number as calculated by his original birth name and by the name that he is more commonly known.

In the first case the calculation can be done by simply adding the Soul and Personality Numbers together, this can be done for the double digit and single digit expressions of his number and the calculation for each is as follows;

Double Digit – 25 + 48 = 73.

Single Digit – 7 + 3 = 10, which is reduced to 1.

Phillip's number is therefore expressed as 73/1. For a full interpretation he would initially examine 1 as a personal vibration number and 73/1 as a more detailed expression of the influences over his life at birth.

As Phillip has, at some point in his life, opted to use his second personal name in its shortened version, rather than Phillip, it is sensible to examine how this may have changed his Destiny number and the influences that will come to play in his life. In this case the calculation would be as follows;

J/1, I/9, M/4, H/8, A/1, L/3, L/3.

1+9+4+8+1+3+3 = 29/11.

Jim's chosen name therefore changes his Destiny number to 29/11 – in this case the 11 is a Master Number and is not therefore reduced to 2. It's interesting to note that in Jim's case his Destiny number using his original name is 1, while this transforms into 11 under his chosen name. Master Numbers tend to have profound influences on our lives and in this example the result of changing his name is, in fact, to intensify the influence of his original birth Destiny Number. 1

is identified with leadership with a focus of benefit for the self as a Destiny Number; however, 11 retains the heavy focus on leadership but with a much greater focus on leadership for the wider good, or for more altruistic purposes. This is a good example of how our Destiny Number can be altered by changing our name but, ultimately the vibrations of those numbers with which we are born will always echo strongly in our lives whatever changes we make. It also serves as a useful example of how it can be important to examine the Destiny Number in relation to original names and later changes.

The Personal Year Number.

Numerology can influence our lives in a number of different ways; you can, for example, simply add up the digits making up today's date to come up with a number that will describe the particular characteristics, influences and challenges that the day may bring. However, this is a broad interpretation of general numerological vibrations and should not dictate how you approach the day! The vibrations of a given day affect us all but not, necessarily, in a profound way. If, however, the day has a number which reflects one of your own personal number combinations, it may be worth considering how beneficial that may be to you in your projects and activities of the day, focusing on the skills and abilities that the number bestows and using them to their full!

The same method can be applied to different months, while the year can also be calculated down to its most significant vibrations, to give you an idea what and who to focus on. However, the most useful way to use Numerology to consider where you should focus your efforts and attentions each year is to calculate your personal year number. To do this simply use the date of your birthday this year.

In the case of our example Jim this would be 06/21/2014 (US format). The calculation is as follows;

6+2+1+2+1+4 = 16/7.

This number, 16/7, can be used by Jim to interpret the particular influences that will fall over his life in the year from his last birthday to his next. The personal year number runs from birthday to birthday and doesn't follow the calendar year, so in Jim's case it would cover half of 2014 and half of 2015, after which a new personal year number would come into force. To interpret the influences of the coming year, Jim would consider the influence of 7 and, again, for the number 16/7 for a more specific understanding of how the number is influencing his year.

Part 2: Personal Number Descriptions

In this section we look in detail at the meanings and vibrations of the single digit numbers. In this first section we'll cover each of the numbers 1-9 and their meanings and influences. You can use this section to develop a basic understanding of how each number vibrates and it's influence on events. Following on from this we will then look more closely at each number as they relate to the four numbers with which we are all endowed.

Number 1.

This is the first number, the original, the divine, the number of inspiration. It is the male principle of creativity and the symbol of unity. 1 is about "me", "I am" and vibrates with a strong sense of power and identity.

Number 2.

Traditionally, 2 represents the female, yang element of the universe. This number represents the duality of the couple, the pair and of cooperative endeavor. It can appear indecisive but is, in fact, the representative of adaptability and of compromise. The vibrations of this number bring together the unity and strength of 1, doubled, when in harmony and in a positive aspect.

Number 3.

This is the combination of the first two numbers. It combines all of their qualities but is about the wider group. This is the number of communication, of society of joy. The qualities of exuberance and sociability are endowed by this number. This number is about the joy of social experience and has a playful aspect.

Number 4.

This number expresses solidity, roundedness and security. It creates strong foundations, stability and it influences construction, building, pragmatic and real matters. It endows practical abilities, sound skills and a strong work ethic.

Number 5.

Note the shape of the number here; the square of four opens from the top with a curling, inquisitive tail. Curiosity is a key principle of this number, it bestows energy, creativity and knowledge. This number falls between the mid-points of the cycle between 1-9. It is a turning point and a point of decision. Change is encapsulated in the essence of this number.

Number 6.

Again, the shape of this number gives us a clue as to its influences. The tail curls inward, creating a closed circle. This is a number that wishes to create balance, to complete, to create harmony and healing. Strongly influencing home, marriage, love and a sense of community, this number is about creating safe spaces – both in a domestic setting and on a wider community level.

Number 7.

A sharp, incisive number, 7 seeks answers. A number of philosophy, silence and introspection are also considered key traits of this number. Questioning requires reflection too and this is part of the influence of number 7. Intellectuals, academics and scientists often fall under the influence of this number.

Number 8.

While 6 moves towards completion and security, 8 represent wholeness, completion and achievement. It has come full circle and assumes power, recognition and financial reward. As an influence 8 drives ambition, successful ventures and maturity. It also encapsulates wisdom, recognition and achievement in the world.

Number 9.

Reflecting 6, 9 opens outward from the safety and security of home, of one's own life and offers solace, compassion and love. 9 gives back in full to the universe all that it has learned. It is often associated with artists and writers but also with religious and spiritual individuals. It is a number which represent selflessness in many guises and a patience, tolerance and love of all.

Life Lesson Numbers and Influences.

Number 1.

Strength of will, a pioneering spirit, creativity and the ability to forge ahead alone are all lessons and attributes that you must learn in life. For those with this number as a life lesson number it's important not to look back. Learn from your experiences but always face forward and look to the future, taking your knowledge and experience with you. Natural careers for those who have this number as a life lesson number are any role in business management. Creative, but with strong administrative abilities, you'll most likely rise to the top if you follow the lessons above. Executives with this number will invariably do well. This number is about creation, initiation and power; the lessons you must learn are to believe in your own abilities to create strong, successful enterprises.

Number 2.

As a Life Lesson Number 2 asks us to learn to mix, to socialize and to work effectively as part of a team. This is not a number of leadership but of support and you must learn to support others in their endeavors. In workplace settings individuals with this number as a Life Lesson number will make good salespeople and negotiators. Diplomats can also learn the lessons this number requires of us. This number teaches you to support, to create solid partnerships and groups. The benefits from this are endless as, although you may not lead, those in power will come to rely on you. Charity or NGO work is often a great field to learn these important life lessons and those with this number as their Life Lesson number will thrive on bringing disparate groups of people together to work for a greater goal.

Number 3.

Learning to have ambition, pride and to be expressive are the lessons that this number requires of us. This number needs us to work out in the world with others and is suited to those working in a wide range of 'social' fields. This can range from government to the arts. The key lesson is to focus on one area and to develop a strong discipline, pride in your completed projects and in your achievements. Artists are often found with this number as a Life Lesson; learning to create and see projects through and to expose them to the wider world is a key lesson. Writing, journalism and teaching are also careers which will help to develop the conscientious and creative energies that this number requires of us.

Number 4.

Stability, certainty and strong foundations are the lessons that this number will bring to your life. You must learn to construct your world from the ground up (this can be literally) and to build your life on strong foundations. In terms of workplaces suited to those born under the influence of this number administrative roles, which require planning and order, or roles in construction and architecture, which have similar requirements are ideal. Those with 4 as a life lesson number need to learn to build equally strong relationships at home. They care deeply for their families and will offer strong, practical support to them. Thrift and diligence are key lessons that this number will require you to learn as you pass through life.

Number 5.

Inquisitive number 5; this number will expect you to get out there and learn new things. Life will be enhanced by frequent travel and frequent learning. Learn to love having new experiences and avoid becoming bound by circumstance, which will lead you to a lack of accomplishment in life. Work which involves dealing with the public is ideal to help you to learn the lessons of this number. Variety, diversity and interaction are key skills to develop. Wide reading is likely to come naturally to you and public speaking, lecturing and work within the publishing world are all likely to appeal to you and benefit you.

Number 6.

This is the number of home, family and love. In the case of the latter this is in a wider sense than just the domestic setting of partnership, or marriage, but indicates compassion and caring for the wider world. You must learn to give much of yourself if this is your life lesson number and to do so to a broad spectrum of people. Learning to balance compassion, understanding and the needs of others is important to you. While the arts can help to learn these lessons careers that are particularly suitable are nursing, medicine, social work or even farming and animal care. Developing compassion for others is the lesson you must learn in life and you will thrive in the happy atmosphere (at home and work) that learning this lesson will create.

Number 7.

The number of deep, philosophical thought and wisdom. These are lessons and skills that you must learn if you have this number as your life lesson number. Intuition is a talent bestowed by this number and it is this intuition which will often lead you to the answers that you seek; as long as you learn to trust it! Academic careers, or those in any spiritual field, will suit those with 7 in their Numerology chart and will be very beneficial to those with it as a life lesson number. Specific areas include science, research and philosophy. Careers where analysis is a key skill are good areas and developing strong analytical skills is crucial for you. Silence, retreat and meditation are also important skills for you to learn; they will help to develop your abilities to think deeply and will be hugely beneficial for you.

Number 8.

This number urges you to lead; it relates strongly to power and to ambition and you should not shy away from either if this is your life lesson number. Your own success is important but helping others to achieve results in their own lives is also significant for you. Any area of business is a good environment for you but you should focus on building strong, successful enterprises. Mentorship is also important to you and you are an excellent leader to offer guidance to others. You can be an excellent motivational speaker but are also likely to have strength and stamina to be successful in sports and also coaching. Learn to be proud but to do so with integrity. Wisdom is also a crucial attribute of this number, learn to develop it early and to be prepared to share it later.

Number 9.

This number expresses love of humanity. Learning to work with, and for, others is crucial if this is your life lesson number. Careers from counseling to statesmanship are suitable places to learn the important lessons this number encapsulates and areas in which you will excel. You will need to build strong family foundations, which will teach you compassion and the ability to share the good things in life. Selfless love is a strong lesson to learn in order to develop your ability to benefit the wider community. Excellent benefactors and leaders are found influenced by this number and while knowledge and wealth will come easily to you, you must learn to share this for a greater good if 9 is your life lesson number.

The Master Numbers as Life Lesson Numbers

The Master Numbers have powerful aspects and if you have one of these as your Life Lesson Number you should consider it as a significant pointer that it is essential for you to learn the lessons they command. Many Numerologists believe that we live many lives, reincarnated to learn all of the lessons that we must understand to achieve a higher state of consciousness. In previous lives your life lesson number may have been all of the numbers described above. If you have a Master Number as your life lesson number it's likely that you have already learned much and must now distill that knowledge and learn it at a much deeper level. All of the Master Numbers have a strong element in which they urge us to help others in wider society, drawing on the key skills of the numbers that they encapsulate.

Number 11.

If 1 is the "me" of numerology then 11 is "us". Reduced it would be interpreted as 2 and, in some senses, it does refine the lessons of this number (and should be read in conjunction with it). Like 1 it also teaches power and leadership but in this case these should be focused for the good of all and not just for the self. This is a number that many who live under its influence will find themselves drawn to matters spiritual. Teach, preach, offer solace, succor and support; this is the message that 11 as a Life Lesson Number is trying to tell you. You will naturally have high standards, a strongly creative approach and a need to see these in others. It's possible with this number that you may find it hard to balance life in a spiritual and material way but this is a lesson that is deeply embedded in the number. Understand that the soul and the body are one and dual at the same time, that both must find sustenance. Using your incredibly strong leadership powers can lead to arrogance and this is a lesson that 11 will require you to understand and to combat.

Number 22.

Again, this number can be seen as distilling many of the qualities of 4, to which it could be reduced. It's also made up of the number 2, which relates to people, love and relationships. In this case, it is more about large groups of people and about building success through practical skills and cooperation. Self-knowledge is important for those with this number in their chart and, in this case, it's self-knowledge that helps you to create strong, lasting structures in the physical world. Large organizations are a good place for those with this as a life lesson number; organizations which build and create real products or deliver tangible results. Either the world of big business or the world of major charity work will be ideal places to learn what this number requires of you. Learning to take charge, know your skills and limits and to create strong structures for the benefit of others in a very broad sense are all encapsulated in this Master Number.

Number 33.

The number 3 is a sociable and gregarious number and 6 (an element of this number) is about community and family. Projects and careers which support the community in general are key areas in which to learn the lessons of this Master Number. Careers which contribute to the welfare of the planet will be a good area in which to focus. Organic farming or renewable technologies help to develop the creative, sociable and caring aspects this number requires to you learn. The arts, particularly music, may be a good choice too. Music requires cooperation, collaboration and the ability to express your emotions along with the ability to move people on an emotional level. Learning to love, in a very wide sense, and benefiting all of those around you are the lessons that this number requires.

Number 44.

Courage and practicality are inherent qualities of this number. Standing firmly and squarely in defense of your principles and backing these up with arguments that are strong are also important elements that this number requires you to learn and develop. 4 brings the high level of solid grounding and strength to those influenced by this number while 8 brings wisdom, power and strong leadership qualities. Combined in this Master Number this is a very powerful set of qualities. The ability to bring justice where there is none and to right wrongs through practical acts is likely to be an important area for you. Working in the legal system or government and regulatory bodies is a good place to put the skills that this number will bestow to their best use and these areas are ones where you will master the life lessons that this number expects of you.

The Soul Number

Number 1.

Individuality and independence are key drivers for you. You will be strong in your beliefs and attitudes, seeking freedom from constriction in all areas of your life. You have a great inner strength and can find it difficult to form close relationships – preferring to rely on yourself. While the strength of character that this number bestows makes you deeply self-reliant, a survivor and not susceptible to manipulation, it can also be destructive in personal relationships or business ones if you allow your inner needs for control and freedom to become too dominant. These characteristics can make you a great leader but an inflexible one if you do not temper them. You will thrive best in situations and careers that give you both freedom of movement and freedom of action.

Number 2.

Tactful, peace loving and seeking harmony in all areas of your life, you will follow rather than take the lead in many situations. You will act as a diplomat in every area of life, building bridges between friends, family and co-workers. You have a strongly developed emotional intelligence and embody tact in all of your dealings in life. Your desire for harmony can lead you to avoid confrontation and mean that you will defer to the wishes of others. This make you appear to lack confidence or can lead to you being dominated in personal relationships. Allowing the influence of this number as a Soul Number to dominate can lead you to become withdrawn, fearful and shy. Developing your instincts and working with others on an equal footing are skills to learn to ensure that you are not trampled by less peace-seeking (and peace-keeping) individuals.

Number 3.

Dutiful and wishing to work for other's benefit, in a broad sense, you'll often find that your strong inspiration and creative abilities, along with your sociable nature will bring many people to your door. Using creative skills you'll bring entertainment to those around you and 3, as a soul number, will make you suitable to work in a whole range of creative industries. You can, however, find that you wish to please everyone all of the time and that you can focus on aiding all around you at your own expense. Happiness for you is found by making others happy. While this is no bad thing, out of control, it can leave you drained emotionally and mentally. Cheerfulness is a trait that is associated with this number and it will be a natural draw to others. Learn to balance the needs of others against your own occasional need to withdraw and listen to your own intuition.

Number 4.

With this number as a driving force of your inner soul you'll be organized, capable and practical. These are useful inner drivers to possess. You are a loyal friend and lover and balanced enough to offer sensible practical support to those around you. You have strong abilities at finding practical solutions to problems in most areas of life and many people will come to rely on you for financial and emotional support. The practicality that this number bestows means that your own life will be built on solid foundations and you'll not be prone to being taken advantage of. Careers in counseling can be a good place to use the skills that this number brings and will be fulfilling for you. Equally, anything where practical, real ends can be achieved will also be areas in which your unique talents can be deployed to great success.

Number 5.

Inquisitive, searching, questioning and with a desire to be continuously on the move are all facets of this number. You will question most things, searching for answers using your intuition and you'll be an insightful individual in most areas of life. Travel will be an essential ingredient in life for you and you quickly become bored if required to stay in one place for too long. This can lead you to a wandering, unsettled life, which can block you from achieving success in some areas of life and may lead others to see you as flighty and unreliable. Feed your restlessness with constant opportunities for travel and learning. Learning that your high energy, quick wit and inability to remain still can be exhausting for others is an important lesson!

Number 6.

Closure, completion, security and stability are all important to those with 6 as a Soul number. Security can become a strong focus and this can be expressed as a need to obtain material wealth and possessions. In relationships it can be overwhelming (as well as comforting) and this is something that you should be aware of and learn to balance. You are deeply affectionate to your close friends and family and constantly seek to offer them the stability that is important to you. Domesticity is important to you and often family is the most important thing to those governed by this number. The biggest danger with this number, particularly for parents, is to be over-protective. Learn to allow your loved ones the space and freedom that they need and express your love in ways which make them feel safe but not smothered.

Number 7.

Thoughtful, intelligent, deeply analytical and a lover of peace and quiet. Those with 7 as their soul number will often be found in the peaceful surroundings of a library, or lost in thought seated in a quiet place in the countryside! With an ability to get straight to the heart of the matter they can seem blunt. These individuals will think deeply before speaking but when that blunt answer suddenly comes from silence people can be shocked! However, problem solving skills on this level are sought after and many will rely on your sound judgment and thoughtful approach. Noisy environments are not always the best for you and many under this influence remain single rather than choose noisy, family life. They will also seek to benefit humanity and the spiritual life may well appeal.

Number 8.

Those falling under the influence of this number may well be driven by ambition. They are also blessed with wisdom and powerful characteristics. Ambition can manifest as stubbornness and obstacles will be tackled with a determination that will amaze others. Organization skills, the development of other's skills and leadership skills will all be driving parts of your personality. Although you may be seen as driven by some, it's likely that you'll also thrive on helping others to achieve their dreams and your skills in this area will be invaluable. You have a deep, instinctive understanding that success in large projects is dependent on everybody working to the best of their abilities and you'll be able to identify and develop these skills in others. Ambition can take over, however, leaving you finding it hard to develop close personal relationships and tempering your competitive nature in this area of life can be useful!

Number 9.

Those for who this is the soul number will be strongly intuitive individuals. With a strong imagination (and consequently prone to day-dreaming) you are also endowed with sympathetic and empathetic skills. You will be driven to help others in all areas of your life, being forgiving and understanding in most circumstances. These abilities can lead to you being taken advantage of by less principled individuals. You are motivated by love of humanity and it's important to remember that this motivation is not one shared by all. You will clearly feel the pain of others and will have a strong desire to ease this pain. Ideally you should work in settings which will allow you to express these abilities and focus these skills. Your company will be widely sought but you should balance this with your strong need for meditation and time alone.

Number 11.

Deeply spiritual and possessing a deep awareness of the life and death cycle you will bring courage, selflessness and strength to your own life and those of people around you. A natural and adept leader you will offer guidance and be a source of strength to many others. You have naturally clairvoyant skills and may find yourself leaning towards spiritual disciplines in life.

Number 22.

Creating lasting structures or organizations which benefit others will be a key focus for you. You are hands on, you wish to create a better world for everybody. These needs can lead to idealism but you have a strong practical grounding and attitude. You should use this to combat idealism taking over your life. You'll not provide leadership, but support and real, solid skills for those in leadership roles. You are reliable, honest and will become a valued "go-to" individual in both personal and work settings. Practical skills will bring practical, material rewards for those governed by this number.

Number 33.

This number combines a sense of protection with a need to serve humanity. It's a number of self-sacrifice and idealism. This can lead you to tirelessly working for the greater good of humanity or to fanaticism. You have a strong ability to envisage a better world but don't always have the practical skills to bring this about. You can, however, communicate clearly – more clearly than many – and you should use these abilities to develop and disseminate your ideas. Your visions are strong and those around you will be willing to take them on-board and develop them with you.

Number 44.

This number expresses itself through a strong desire (and ability) to lead, combined with a deeply practical and accomplished soul. You seek out learning, knowledge, wisdom and then turn them to leading others. Your problem solving skills are second to none and you have the personal presence to both encourage others to take on your solutions and to believe in you. Leadership in government roles, or in high level diplomatic posts, are ideal ways in which you can combine your inner drives and your outer accomplishments. You have a strong sense of your own abilities and this, on occasion, can express as arrogance or pride.

The Outer Personality Number

Number 1.

Strongly independent and possibly perceived as a "loner", 1 projects an aura of difference. A leader not a follower, people with this number as their personality number easily find followers as they are seen as not only different but capable, and able to control any situation. Whether it's a local club, or a multi-national organization, those under the influence of this number will always be found close to the top – probably right at the top! The independent and forthright nature that this number projects can come across as aggressive, domineering and opinionated.

Number 2.

The personality that this number projects is quiet, often perceived as shy, retiring and accommodating when it comes to others' needs. Preferring to not make a big impression this personality is, however, popular and always ready to offer help, support, love to others. Neat, fastidious and fond of balance in all areas of life you can, on occasion, appear indecisive as you can always see both sides of an argument. You are very flexible in your efforts to achieve harmony but this can be perceived as being easy to manipulate.

Number 3.

The personality projected by this number is outgoing, fun-loving, garrulous and extrovert. People are naturally drawn to your charm, your sense of fun and your naturally sociable character. Your communication abilities are strong and you love to be the center of attention. Generally people with this number as their personality number have a wide circle of friends and associates. You will often been seen as expressive and creative but where the traits are too strong you may be viewed as gossipy, shallow and others may be jealous of your popularity and abilities. You value wit and openness in others and mix well in any social setting.

Number 4.

The practical no-nonsense attitude that this number projects is the strongest impression you will create amongst others. They will see you as grounded, down to earth and pragmatic. You will often come across as work orientated, valuing hard work above all else. These traits will help you to achieve much in life but can lead to the impression that you have no real time for play. You may be seen as very traditional, focusing on home and country as the most important things in life. You will project an image of frugality but this may be seen as being mean and you may appear simply too practical for some people, which can lead you to becoming isolated. People projecting this personality are nearly always well-dressed in good quality clothes – quality being important to them. Often perceived as reserved, you can sometimes be viewed as cold.

Number 5.

Active, changeable, hugely inquisitive and in need of constant stimulation from new sources. This number can mean that you'll appear vital, interesting and filled with energy and enthusiasm for life. You can also appear to become bored easily and will often seek stimulation in new places and with new groups of friends. This can lead to other people seeing you as 'false' or 'fickle'. Often people with this number expressing their outer personality will not settle for life with one partner but have multiple relationships through their lives. You will also be seen as a risk taker and a persuasive individual. However, the downsides of your personality can lead to the perception that you are restless, unreliable and cannot be depended upon.

Number 6.

Home loving and protective are the two significant attributes that this number projects. You will find that people are drawn to you as a confidante and will often find yourself teaching, helping or counseling others. Social justice and charity work are important to you and these will be seen as a big part of your life. This can lead you to interfere in the lives of others rather too much – which can break relationships and cause resentment. You love balance and are often drawn to the arts, which will lead you to be viewed as both a connoisseur and an expert in this area. People will naturally be drawn to your impeccable taste in art, clothes and material objects and also to the protective, nurturing qualities that you display.

Number 7.

Mysterious, a seeker of solitude, something of a loner and also deeply intelligent. The personality that this number projects can be hard for others to approach. You may find that your air of spirituality and your philosophical approach to life keep people at arm's length. If this outer personality is in conflict with your soul number then you should make efforts to be open with those around you about your true nature. People with this number as their outer personality number rarely display interest in material possessions and often give a sense of "otherness" and enigma. While these qualities can be daunting there is something wise in their air and something that inspires deep trust. Appearing highly analytical, this number can also appear obsessive!

Number 8.

A strong, executive and powerful presence emanate from those who are under the influence of this number. Physically and emotionally you also seem to be possessed with endless reserves of energy. This number creates a sense of leadership and you'll find that people are eager to follow you. This sense can be destructive if it leads you to abuse that power. This is an ambitious number and you'll dislike being crossed in your ambitions. People may perceive this as cruelty – which it can be if you don't control these urges. However, this number bestows qualities that will also make you keen to help others achieve their goals and many will come to you for help for just that purpose – your own personal qualities proving valuable to them in this field.

Number 9.

Gentle, friendly and full of charm, people are drawn to you as you seem to have a wealth of experience and understanding. This is a gentle but all-knowing personality full of wise words and compassion. Your humanity and generosity are also noticeable and attractive, though not always for the best of motives as people may take advantage of both. You can be too sensitive to the pain of others and this can lead you to a depth of sadness (not self-pity) that others do not experience. You may become withdrawn and depressed as a result and need to recognize the importance of time away from others as well as time helping them.

The Master Numbers

Number 11.

Visionary, unique, independent and yet protective of all of those around you – people under the influence of this number are often artistic, creative and achieve great success in these fields. Recognition is likely to come your way often – in small and large ways. You will be seen as inspirational by others and this will lead people to follow your example in many areas of life. Idealism is a key trait of this number and it can, if not tempered, lead to a self-centered approach to life, which is detrimental to your talents. In all areas of your life you will display a unique, original approach which can be both inspiring but also eccentric!

Number 22.

Combining diplomacy with practicality this number suggests a person who is not only sensitive to the needs of others but also practical at dealing with the world. This number suggests somebody who is able to make real changes in the world – for better or worse. There is a strong sense of a need to serve the world in a wider sense and many great diplomats, past and present, have been under the influence of this number. Dangers to be aware of with this number are a tendency to use any means necessary to achieve a goal – which can lead to accusations of corruption or dishonesty. On occasion these accusations can be based on fact!

Number 33.

Generous beyond measure, humble and always ready to help are the attributes that this number will project. You never seem to expect anything in return for your efforts (which are many) and people in great need will be drawn to you. You seem to have natural abilities with young children and animals, in particular, and may work in a field which allows you to utilize these skills. People may view you as self-sacrificing and this is often true. The largest danger with this number is that you will take self-sacrifice to the extreme and may also be used by others with less positive intentions. This can lead you to displaying a sense of martyrdom.

Number 44.

Disciplined, to the point of seeming military, you will exude a sense of quiet strength. You give off a profound sense of purpose, determination and clarity, which some can find deeply reassuring, while others may find daunting. You can be immensely practical and ambitious, capable of achieving your desires against any odds. You may seem to be so practical that you appear to be constantly working and stuck in a rut as a result. Smart, efficient and capable people with this number as their outer personality number will often be found working for the authorities (military, police, security etc). While you are good at giving, or taking orders, you will rebel if you can see no practical reason for them; at this point you can be devastatingly crushing.

The Destiny Number

Number 1.

"I am" is a key phrase of this number. You are here to put yourself first and to learn to do so. Your desires and needs will come first in life, other people can look after themselves. There is nothing wrong with caring for yourself and ensuring your own needs are met but you must be careful of selfishness – which will not ultimately benefit you! This destiny is about learning who you are, learning to lead others and learning to be self-reliant. Do not be afraid to live your own life in the way that you see fit and be prepared to avoid the constraints of conventionality.

Number 2.

A naturally tactful, calm and caring individual you will seek to create balance and harmony in all situations. This number teaches us to work with others, to create balance and peace. You will also have a sense of duality, of opposites and be able to learn to reconcile these. This number can lead to indecisiveness and this is an important lesson for you to learn – how to balance different arguments and practicalities to create the perfect solution and to then move forward. You may need to learn to put yourself second in order to support and develop others around you.

Number 3.

You have a destiny to inspire others; you may choose to do this in a wide range of careers or life paths. Expression and communication are your tools and you must learn to use these well. It's likely you'll choose a field which allows you to communicate broadly. Languages will appeal to you and you should learn as many as you can! The naturally garrulous and love for company that this number embodies can lead you to have too many interests and too wide a circle of friends and acquaintances. You must learn to use your talent to inspire in a measured way which results in benefits for yourself and others and doesn't just lead you to burn out.

Number 4.

You will find that you have a strong need to construct real things in the world and things that are of practical use. This is not the number of an artist – although design will be a strong draw to you. You need to combine your practical skills with your creative ones and develop these to create real and sustainable results. You will be drawn to hard work and be highly productive. People with this destiny number are hardworking, practical, patient and loyal. They can become dogged, or work against the odds, although often they will achieve success where others would have failed. You will expect others to be obedient and may domineer on occasion.

Number 5.

Your life will be filled with change, movement and inspiration. This can be fulfilling and it can be exhausting. Your destiny is to learn to adapt to change and to lead others in doing so. You will naturally rebel against "old-fashioned" ways of thinking and acting and will often work to overturn outdated ideas or create new ways of doing things. Sometimes this can lead to "change for change's sake" and you must learn to also accept that some things do still work! You have an inquiring, analytical mind and should learn to use this to evaluate. You'll find yourself in new situations frequently and should learn to use these as a chance for growth and self-development.

Number 6.

Home and family will feature first and foremost throughout your life. A natural "nest-builder" you will seek out comfort and pleasure but mainly as a benefit for those that you love.

Naturally proud of your family and their achievements, you will also be a good socializer, enjoying good company and creating a welcoming atmosphere. You have a keen eye for detail and can create not only a beautiful home but would work well as an event organizer – or in any field where you can bring together your natural talents for creating a safe environment. You will be able to read people well and will be a source of support for many around you but will be most protective of your own family. You must learn that, while this is positive, it must not be allowed to become domineering or suffocating.

Number 7.

You are a seeker after the truth and an explorer of mysteries. You must learn to love your own company and will often prefer to be alone, studying, looking or simply thinking. Your incisive mental qualities are a key part of your nature and you may need to learn to use these for the benefit of others. Researchers, scientists and philosophers will often fall under the influence of this number and these paths will suit you well. You have strong mental powers but also seek a deeper truth and may be drawn to spirituality in one way or another. This is a path which will bring out your best qualities and is one that may be perfect for you.

Number 8.

Endowed with strength and courage beyond the norm, perseverance is also one of your key attributes. Your path may not be easy in life – certainly not at first - but you must learn to use your own inner resources to overcome obstacles. You will be driven by a sense of ambition and will seek success in life. You may do so at the expense of others but you must learn that your own skills are valuable and can be shared with others. The sheer stamina that this number endows offers great potential in the sporting field and your ability to motivate will also offer strong possibilities in this area. Your destiny is to succeed but you will do this through learning and wisdom; listen to your inner self for guidance, it will help you to achieve great things in the world.

Number 9.

You will meet many trials and tribulations in life in your search for peace, perfection and progression. You will often seek to help others achieve peace and your natural skills will aid you in this. Your goal in life will be to leave the world in a better state than it was when you entered it. This is the number of the philanthropist, the humanitarian, the benefactor. Spirituality will be an important part of your life but you will need to share your knowledge and wisdom with others. The change and improvement that you seek for humanity can take many generations to achieve and, to avoid disillusion and bitterness, you must learn to recognize that you are only a part of the solution and that even small changes can make a big difference in the end. Altruism is a big part of your personality and you will often be recognized for this.

The Master Numbers

Number 11.

This number bestows great creative potential. It is also a number associated with individuality and insight (on an almost psychic level). It is the number of the visionary and it will lead you to a path of expression and individuality which is likely to lead to fame (and/or notoriety). You have real prophetic abilities and you also desire to improve life for others. These can be hard qualities to live with as, seeing the broader picture can lead you to see the darker side of life too clearly. Avoid feelings of pessimism and disenchantment and be sure that your unique skills can lead you to a position of great power and influence.

Number 22.

You will be a naturally confident leader and will almost certainly seek to achieve a position of power. You will look to become wealthy in life and will probably succeed. You'll often be drawn to public life, or to the corporate world. While deeply materialistic, you'll seek to build structures and organizations that benefit many people. Your leadership qualities have a deeply practical aspect to them; you like to be "hands-on" and this can lead to being too involved in details. You will work hard in life and expect others to do exactly the same. You may be frustrated by those who appear less committed to success than yourself or those who are more "cerebral" in their approach to life.

Number 33.

Born to serve and born to feel the pain of humanity. This is a hard path to live but one which will allow you to create real change. Injustice and suffering cut you to the core of your being and you will fight for the rights of others above your own. Strongly expressive and a powerful speaker you will be able to illustrate clearly the wrongs and woes that you seek to set right. This is a number that makes you a campaigner and will also heap burdens upon you. You should learn to respond to these needs and take them on – it will provide you with a sense of fulfillment. Avoid feelings of being a martyr as these will be destructive to your core destiny.

Number 44.

Logical, and with practical skills to put that logic to applied solutions, you will be an ambitious leader and a wise counselor. Serving the world around you in a practical way is a core attribute of this number and it will bring you fulfillment in both material and spiritual ways. You will build on a practical level but also on an intellectual level, always desiring to create practical solutions that benefit the wider world. This personality will be capable of running whole countries or rebuilding fractured communities. People will seek you out for the wisdom you embody, the practical abilities that are so clear and forcefulness of your personality.

Part 3: Double Digit Influences and Descriptions

When we calculate the numbers that represent our four personal numbers we find that we may come to a double digit number. For example, a personal number of 5 may be the result of a calculation that combines 1 and 4 or 3 and 2 either as 14, 41, 32 or 23. While the basic numbers are the most significant, the way in which the combinations work on us is more subtle and is expressed in these double digit numbers.

This can give us a more complex understanding of the forces acting upon and for this reason it's useful to examine these combinations. Going back to our example of Phillip James Hall, the soul number was expressed as 25/7. In this case the 2 is working with the 5 to create 7. While 4 and 3 would have the same result the means through which this result is achieved would have slightly different connotations.

In this example 2 is a number of duality, of diplomacy and tact; 5 is inquisitive and restless, 7 represents philosophy, knowledge, great intellect and strength but also a certain level of isolation from others. For Phillip (or Jim, as it turns out!) these will difficult attributes to balance in life and he can develop an deeper understanding of his own, inner personality by exploring these different facets that influence him.

The four different personal numbers that we all have (five if you count the possible alternative reading for someone who changes their name and may alter their destiny number by doing so) all act on us in different ways (the soul number being our inner self, the outer personality being what we project and the destiny representing what we must learn to be etc). Bearing this in mind, you can use the following descriptions to see how the combination affects the relevant part of your life or those who you are creating a reading for. In this Part we look at the Double Digit combinations only as 1-9 are covered earlier in the book.

Double Digit Descriptions.

10/1.

You will find that luck and success come your way easily. You have a deep understanding of your own nature and may feel you have lived before and learned much about yourself. You are unique, you have much to teach those around you and stand out as a strong individual with a depth of inner resources beyond the norm. You like to see your plans succeed and may have many of these. You will, however, take one thing at a time, working to achieve success and then moving on to the next goal. You are very much in touch with yourself and this inner power expresses itself in the outer world, often creating reverence, respect and a little fear amongst others.

11/2.

Although 11 is one of the Master numbers it's useful to explore the vibrations that it also contains as a component number of 2. This combination gives deeply intuitive powers; you experience a sense of consciousness beyond the self and can draw on a deep level of universal knowledge. You may experience clairvoyance or prophetic dreams. You can also be idealistic and the number 11 will give you great leadership powers. At the same time the ability to work to achieve balance is incredibly important to you. Legal work will appeal to you, especially that which promotes social justice. While you seek to benefit others and may shy from leadership you will actually excel at the latter and may receive great recognition or reward for your effort.

12/3.

This number is where 1 and 2 become 3. It is in many cases a number that begets a strange personality. You'll incorporate individuality with a centered, balanced nature and the ability to get along with everybody you meet. Others will seek you for guidance, insight and peace and you will be able to deliver this clearly and with lucidity. You not only have a deep connection with your spiritual and intuitive side but with the wider, material world. This can make you seem odd to others, seeking both spiritual peace and material, worldly pleasure. This is however the sign of a deeply evolved spirit who understand that the needs of the body and the mind must both be met in order to achieve balance. 12 is a number that represents experience (think the 12 signs of the zodiac) while the 3 represents youthfulness and sociability. This explains why people with this combination are at one and the same time deeply (anciently) wise and youthful, fun-loving at the same time. You can be an enigma to others but will retain a deep serenity within yourself.

13/4.

Esoterically 13 is viewed to represent "Death" but this is a widely mis-held misconception. Symbolically it is better described as a state of change. For the practical, constructive 4 this number influences them in just that way. They build in order to change, they destroy in order to build or create something better. 13 will reverberate through your life by causing changes to be frequent. You may find that whenever you have found peace through creating something new, you will find changes in your life which mean you must now move on to the next project. Change and transformation are key elements of this combination and lost causes can be revived and given new life by those under the influence of this number. They may also be destroyed if they have no practical use! This is a powerful combination and can be expressed in both positive and negatives ways. Stagnation is deathly for those under this vibration and should be avoided at all costs.

14/5.

Inspired practicality combining to create an inquiring, restless soul. The 1 here expresses individuality and clarity of view, the 4 real, practical skills and the 5 needs constant stimulation. Writers, journalists and investigators may find these numbers in their charts. This number bestows a truly vivid imagination but one that understands realities of life. It can create "real" worlds on paper or screen. There is a strong pull to the sensual with this number and those born under its influence can quite literally exhaust themselves through exploration of the sensual pleasures of the world. This should be guarded against as it may lead to a jaded, bored outlook. New ideas and objects will be equally important to you and a strong need to experience the new for yourself will drive you. This number needs a mix of intellectual and practical pursuits and finding the right balance (without overdoing either) will be essential.

15/6.

This number brings an ability to assimilate knowledge in both an academic and emotional way. An excellent student, in life you seek to acquire knowledge in order to create stability, wealth and comfort. You may develop a strong need for status and the trappings of wealth and security (which are well within your capabilities to achieve) but you may use your intellect and understanding of other's emotions to manipulate your way to these ends. Because material comfort, security and the home are important to you may take obstacles and set-backs as serious personal threats. Learn to laugh in the face of difficulties and to work with others constructively to achieve success.

16/7.

This can be a difficult number and path to fall under the influence of. Yet it can also be extremely powerful. 1 is the number of the individual, 6 of the family and security. 1 seeks independence and cares little for convention, 6 seeks peace and harmony. Together they create the 7 which is deeply philosophical with an incisive intellect and wit. Learning and truth are important but there is a strong emotional element to the combination. Those who have the influence in one of their numbers may experience many material and financial challenges, some which they may have brought on themselves through a conflict within. Learning to act in accordance with the needs of all of these different motivations is key to developing the magnetism and force that 7 eventually embodies. Inspiration and understanding of the self and the world often come in a flash of knowledge – a flash that can be blinding and destructive or brilliant and illuminating.

17/8.

Intuitive, scientific, a solver of mysteries. This combination brings together inspiration, depth of thought and a high level of wisdom. Your intellect will be where you start to solve problems but a deeper knowledge will bring you solutions. This is probably the best number to be influenced by if you are a detective! Isolation, meditation and peace are also strong requirements that this number will bring to you. You must withdraw frequently to find the answers that you'll seek. The questions may have importance to others or simply to you. When you have the answers, however, they'll leave you with a much greater understanding of the world around you and, after all, knowledge is power. Stubborn, doubting and sometimes pessimistic, you should seek to dispel these traits through active research and learning.

18/9.

Intensely emotional with a vivid inner life and also a very physically active person is the type denoted by this combination. You are deeply attuned to dreams and may find that this provide you with a great deal of understanding. In this case the 1 and 8 combine intuition and wisdom which means you may act on hunches (correctly) more than other people. This gives you an uncanny ability to get things right first time and to find that obstacles evaporate as you approach. Conquest is important to you and you enjoy physical activity which contains an element of this (climbing high mountains, swimming large lakes, running long distances!). Mountaineering in particular may appeal and distance sports which require physical stamina will be good for you. Your love of benefiting humanity is naturally strong and you'll work in all of your endeavors in this cause. Your intuition and mental abilities are actually fed by your physical health and this is an important aspect to remember.

19/1.

Leadership is innate to 1 and service is innate to 9. Public service in government, or even the military, is a perfect path for those under the influence of this number. Leadership here is sought through the ability to inspire and serve and this path is one that creates a local government leader, a prime minister or a president. In a corporate setting you'll also do well and find yourself at the top. Endurance comes with this combination, physical and mental, both drawn from hidden inner resources. You'll work tirelessly to achieve great results for those you serve. This personal power and leadership is an attractive combination and you'll attract both wealth and inspire love in many.

20/2.

Life will be full of decisions for those falling under this number. The cycle will be repetitive and may be frustrating. This number must achieve balance and do so through analysis of the facts. Along with decisions, you'll find that life constantly offers you choices. Again, it's essential that you learn to make balanced decisions. All of this creates a life in which challenge and change are constant features and, as the ultimate decision maker, you have the power to have a great impact on the world around you. Controlling that world is important to you and beware of the danger of becoming too controlling in personal relationships.

21/3.

This is a combination which bestows luck, success and charm. You express traits of organization, accuracy and openness. Patience is another crucial part of this number and using patience, organization and natural talent you'll find yourself in a popular position in many areas of your life. Expression is another aspect of this number and artists in many different fields have this combination within their charts. They combine the analytical skills of the 2 with the inspiration of 1 and the resulting communicative skills are demonstrated by the 3. Planning, executing and sharing the results will come naturally to you. Success, while not assured with this combination, is highly likely.

22/4.

The Master Number 22 can also be expressed as 4. In this case it indicates wealth and prosperity based on real solid foundations. You will use the resources around you to great effect; these resources can include other people. 22 suggests great abilities at solving problems; you'll analyze well and find it easy to come to solutions. Problems that others have found impossible will be solved with little apparent effort by you. When you have the solution you'll also know how to find the resources to put it into action. This number may be found in the chart of engineers and innovative builders but it can also be found in those working in a wider range of fields including surgery and a medical setting. Making things work, or making them work again, is what you do best.

23/5.

Agile, a love of connecting with others and a nature that needs to explore new places. Physical strength is often a feature of this combination along with the stamina to go with it. While this may suggest athletes and sporting heroes, the energy of this number is more subtle. Communication of complex ideas is a key part of the number and also exposure to the public.

PR and communications roles often will be a great setting to utilize these skills. There is a fieriness to this personality – one that can flare up suddenly but it only an expression of a natural honesty and exuberant energy. It's worth learning to control this in some settings, however! A need for, and love of, change is no bad thing but learning to ensure that each new project and challenge develops you in some way is important.

24/6.

Well balanced and intrinsically practical with a love of home and family. This combination bodes well for a successful, secure future. Home is important but balance and happiness are also key here. You'll enjoy material comfort and have all the necessary skills to achieve a real, tangible sense of this. You may enjoy showing it off but your pride is often most apparent in the achievements of those who you support (your family). Those with this combination make good partners in any sense (business or domestic) and will work to achieve results through practical means. Completion of projects is important to you and you'll see things through however many obstacles may come your way. This combination is about material success in the world – but for all the right reasons!

25/7.

While 2 is deeply analytical, 5 expresses a more intuitive knowledge. 7 itself encapsulates problem solving and incisive thinking. Overall the characteristics of this combination work well to create an individual who is highly intelligent. This intelligence is, however, not simply through academic resources (although they will be important to you) but through gut feeling. The number describes well the brilliant mind who has an emotional intelligence as well. Attention to detail and well developed observational skills all combine in this number to leave others with a sense that you are clairvoyant or psychic. Your mind is constantly alert and seeks constant stimulation. This can lead you to be restless and can often give you a strong need to move on to pastures new on an intellectual level. You may need to learn to focus your efforts more discerningly and find subjects or projects that allow you lots of stimulation without a need to drop them mid-way through in search of the new!

26/8.

This number is one of challenge; you may face numerous problems which must be resolved in order to find success. You must learn from experience if this number is in your chart. However, you'll be motivated by a strong desire for power, for domination and control. You will normally understand that these can only be achieved through analysis and through perseverance. There is something impulsive in this combination and this may be a trait to be aware of. Learn to look before you leap and examine the options as, once you've committed to a project, you'll not settle until it is completed. The wisdom you develop through this process will, in the end, prove your strongest asset. While careers in which your skills are useful are wide, teaching, lecturing or passing on knowledge in any setting, will be good for you.

27/9.

2 brings a search for balance, combined with the ability to see both sides of an argument while 7 brings an incisive intellect. The combination creates a powerful intuitive nature which can take you far in life. The mind in this case is creative, sharp and able to find more than one solution and also to use any of them. This number also brings with it the need to help others and the ability to accept people as they are. You are idealistic in some senses about the world but able to accept others openly. Your intuition means that you are less vulnerable than most to manipulation and can often manipulate rather well, yourself! You may be deeply interested in spiritual matters but will be most interested in the help and healing they can bring to others. This number can represent a missionary, a diplomat or a business leader.

28/1.

This number combines ambition, leadership, inspirational and diplomatic qualities. Here the 2 acts as a foundation for the wisdom and ambition encapsulated in the 8, while the reduced number brings inspirational creativity and individuality. Never fooled by preconceived ideas you can quickly understand how things really work. You can quickly evaluate any situation and see how to take control of it. This number has a great deal of vitality to it. The success that it suggests is built not only on your own abilities but by being able to understand those of others around you. You may use others to achieve success but you'll be fair in doing so and help them to benefit as well. This number is fast to act and can be reckless and can trust (or overestimate) others too quickly.

29/11.

As 29 reduces to 11 (a Master Number) we do not reduce it further to 2. However, those with this number should also read the description for that number as it is encapsulated within the combination on several levels. This can be a number of challenge and test. Boundless energy is found in this combination and the ability to see very clearly both the realities of this world and beyond. Visionary, mystical and yet with a desire (and ability) to succeed in the real, practical world. While 2 (the base number in this combination) is not a leadership number, 11 most definitely is. This can lead you to an inner conflict which you must learn to resolve and also to develop a way in which you can take the lead when necessary but support when this is required. Again, choices and decisions will dominate your life. Accessing your deeper, spiritual self, will be an important part of how you address these matters. Learn to look beyond yourself and then lead others on the best path.

30/3.

A trinity of gifts will be yours in life. The ability to express yourself, an ease at acquiring material success and an ability to reach out to others. You will always seek perfection and may fall short of your own expectations, though others will easily see your brilliance. Center stage is a natural place for you although this stage could be one in a theatrical sense or the operating theater. Your need for perfection means that you will throw yourself into any career with enthusiasm and achieve that central role, in whatever field. Your natural ability to communicate means that a secondary role as a teacher may appeal later in life. Material success is easy for you but you may turn your back on it and seek spiritual knowledge at some point in your life.

31/4.

Outgoing, individual and practical; this number is also highly competitive. You work amongst many people and have to be the best! Your practical skills will set you on the right path to achieve dominance but the influences in this number can not only be competitive but combative. You may have to fight your corner on many occasions and will feel passionately about doing this. A soldier may find themselves with this number in their chart and anyone with this combination must be capable of standing up for themselves. One lesson that this number requires of us is that nobody is an island; cooperation along with competition will help you achieve real, practical results. This is the number of an individual who can work with others to create great results.

32/5.

This number is associated with love – in the sense of a dutiful love. You wish to bring people together in peace and to reach out to the world. You have the strongest sense of duty and a need to serve. This number is found denoting great spiritual leaders and prophets. Its purpose is to draw the world together and create harmony. Charity and work with the disadvantaged will appeal to you strongly and can offer the opportunities that the 5 element (a need for change and travel) will demand. Thanks to the nature that you express help will often come your way, help to achieve projects which benefit others. Material success is unlikely to interest you, unless you can use it to improve the lot of people around you. You will often find yourself stood at a crossroads, with the courage to choose the right way ahead and a lot of people willing to follow you. There are times where this can lead to a sense of (and accusations of) superiority and it's important to be aware of this in your life.

33/6.

As with all numbers containing 3 there is element of wider social understanding in this Master Number. In this case it is a self-sacrificing need to save others. This can be a deeply challenging number and one which requires you to give much of yourself to others. You seek wholeness and completion – mainly for others – and will make a great teacher or speaker. You may often find that tasks of great importance are assigned to you and positions of great (and terrifying) responsibility. Humanitarian work will be important to you – probably something, in fact, that you will be unable to avoid. You have all the energy and courage that you need to rise to the challenges you face but you may find that thanks does not readily come your way. This can affect you negatively and lead to anxiety, exhaustion and regret. It is important to find the role which allows you to improve the world and one that you are happy to take on with little or no thanks.

34/7

This number encapsulates development. Again, as with other 3 numbers this is about development for all. However, you seek practical solutions to problems. Creating better living conditions for others may well suit you in order to create lives where harsh practicalities are removed to give time for learning or development of different kinds. You aim to improve the world and you understand that material wealth, spiritual wealth and intellectual wealth are all necessary for others. You make practical solutions in other's lives to make this possible. Often this number will mean that spirituality is a founding part of your personality and you are introspective as well as deeply practical. You need time alone to come to theoretical solutions and work best on practical projects when doing so with groups. Conflict can distress you because you see it as unpractical and therefore lacking use.

35/8.

Wealth and power often accompany this number and may be inherited. This is also a sociable number and you will enjoy working with others and playing with them as well. Constant change feeds your soul and you'll not be fond of living a settled life, luckily you will often you'll find the funds to travel will be at your disposal. A wide and changing social circle is important to those with this number in their chart and this can mean that the business world attracts them. Wealth and power will also draw you to business and success will be easy. Your naturally inquisitive nature will also be a big driver and this inquisitiveness may lead you to pry and gossip more than is good for you!

36/9.

These three numbers all embody a great deal of strength individually, and combined that power is multiplied. Strong people often have to carry heavy, difficult loads and if your life is ruled by this combination that is almost certainly going to be the case. You'll be a repository of secrets belonging to others, you'll have to protect many people and support them. Often this can be emotionally and financially draining. Luckily you will find the strength and resources to do so within yourself. Intuition and inspiration are embedded in this combination and you'll always know when somebody needs help and also how to provide that help. You will, as your reward, be surrounded by love in life and you will return this love willing. Your view of life will generally be rounded and you will never approach people with preconceptions or a negative frame of mind. You will be required to give much in life but you will receive as much back in the longer term.

37/1.

This number is loving, reserved and mature in its basic elements. Individual, creative, inspirational and communicative it may often be found in the charts of those who work in the arts. They often demonstrate a commanding personality (and do like to be in a position of power). This can be domineering sometimes but generally this number combination suggests a love of people. Although reserved and quiet in some circumstances, the quick wit and desire to inspire respect found in you will make you deeply popular and well loved by many. You can communicate new ideas well and will often feel the need to express yourself in images rather than words. You also draw on the experience of others, analyzing these and expressing them in new ways.

38/11.

This expression of the Master Number 11 brings visionary power, abundance and widespread exposure. You have the power to make intangible dreams real, to earn security and material wealth from your own inspirational ideas and to enthuse others with real passion for your ideas. A creator, inventor and initiator are the roles that you will fulfill. You see beyond the apparent and the physical to other realms and you understand the needs of wider social groups instinctively. You can provide solutions to problems that others have not recognized and this puts you in a unique position. Where you achieve wealth, which is likely, you'll fully enjoy the benefits; however, as you have a need to benefit others with everything you have, charity and philanthropic work will become important to you as you grow older.

39/3.

The philosopher who must serve all is a good way to look at this combination. Although gentle and accepting you desire change to benefit the world around you. You will often be surrounded by people and this is comfortable for you – though you will prefer to listen than talk on many occasions. Your gentle, poetic nature draws many people to you who wish to learn from your broad understanding of the world. Your knowledge is often deep and you are selfless in sharing it. Teachers and spiritual leaders are often found with this combination. Where you find injustice you will, despite your generally gentle nature, fight fiercely to combat it. Statuesque, when crusading for the greater good, you provide inspirational and yet humble leadership for others. When you take on a cause it will nearly always succeed.

40/4.

This number will manifest in order; everything about your life will be ordered to the finest degree. Some may find this obsessive (it can express in this way) or controlling. However, for you it is necessary for everything to not only have a place but to be in that place. Methodical and analytical, you build strong structures in your life. This means strong relationships, strong homes, strong careers, strong foundations for wealth and success. Your planning is so meticulous that it's unlikely you'll fail in these endeavors. There may be a rigidity to your thinking but you may need the structure this provides. Obstacles can appear in your life frequently – these will, however, be removed by a slow and steady process until you can move forward. You are reliable, dependable and known for doing what you say and achieving what you promise; this is the foundation of your success.

41/5

In this aspect the desperate desire for change that is often encapsulated by the number 5 is tempered by the practical inspiration that 41 brings. You'll find that you constantly initiate change yourself, as you are an inspirational and original thinker. However mad the project or unlikely it may seem you bring your practical skills and abilities to the task. The sharp and creative mind that this number bestows means that a life filled with change can be lived in one single location. Your creativity knows no bounds and you exude love, happiness and fun. Many people with this number combination produce large families with lots of children – they like variety after all! Your natural need for pleasure of a practical kind can make you too sensual, on occasion, and avoiding over-indulgence is one essential challenge you may face.

42/6.

The number 6 expressed in this way drives a need to bring peace by practical means. Service to others is often a key trait found in this personality. While this can be the home and family the combination will thrive when that service is devoted to a much wider social group. Social workers, nurses or psychologists may find this number in their chart as their desire to heal and provide safety is strong. You have a natural ability to express emotion and to create a happy atmosphere in any location. Those under the influence of this number do not thrive working alone, nor for purely financial gain. The benefit must be to others and any role in which you serve others is likely to bring out the best in you. Your home is likely to be important to you and you will create a loving, safe space for those who share it with.

43/7.

Gentle, generous and gregarious; also slightly goal orientated. This last aspect of your personality will be well hidden but strong. You combine clarity of thought with practicality of action and a desire to be amongst people. Healers are amongst those who have this number in their chart. You may find that working with those who are less privileged than you also appeals. You provide a high level of inspiration to those around you, who will willing follow your example. While you like to be center of attention, on many occasions, you have strongly developed listening skills. This can, in fact, make you the center of attention more often than talking skills. You can bring a constructive approach to most areas of life and you will often put others first, although this will lead to significant personal and financial rewards in your own life.

44/8.

This number brings with it the desire to be at the top, to be in control and to be respected. While all of that may come in time, you will need to work hard for it. This is not a number which brings power and influence quickly but one which requires slow, steady progress to achieve your results. Logical thinking is one of your key attributes and you apply logic to all areas of your life. This can make you cautious and you'll take time to make decisions, although once made you'll act on them with precision. Intuition is not your strongest skill and those who possess it may puzzle you; you need firm, rational facts before you act. While this may mean your progression in life is slower than that of others it does mean that your success is built on the most firm foundations possible.

45/9.

This number brings with it a contradiction. You have great practical abilities through which you can achieve significant material success. You have a searching, inquisitive nature that allows you to find answers and solutions to questions and problems. You then have the practical skills to make those solutions real. You have all the requirements for quickly building a strong material success in life. Yet this is not enough for you; material success is simply not what your soul is seeking. You have a deep, inner emotional world which does not show itself to others and this can mean you appear as a puzzle. You can be reserved and unwilling to share this side of yourself with others as it embarrasses your naturally practical instincts. Learning to balance your spiritual self with your practical self is a must; suppressing either will leave you feeling (and seeming) dull, uninspired and usually unsuccessful in life. Periods of meditation and withdrawal can be crucial, while physical exercise can help you to explore the physical world that you also love.

46/1.

This combination is extremely strong and very much a dominating personality. Practical, with a strong sense of loyalty to home, family, country and community, it's also a forcefully individual and strident combination. You will be widely popular, considered inspirational and will command both fear and loyalty at the same time. Strong willed, idealistic and intense, while people are inspired by you they may find you unapproachable; you may tend to see this as weakness and be dismissive. Learn to temper you need to dominate with a gentler approach. Your naturally practical skills will help and they will also make you likely to be financially successful in life. Leadership is natural to this number and that leadership in a military setting can often be perfect for that combination of protective strength and natural ability to dominate.

47/11.

Inherent conflict can be found between the deeply practical and deeply emotional aspects that make up this Master Number. Life may be full of contradiction for you and you may feel many emotions intently while your practical nature urges you to move away from them. The secret for success is to set goals for yourself. The vibration of 11 bestows great strength, intuition and insight. Once you have identified a goal you will find your practical nature can combine with your emotional intellect to solve any obstacle you encounter. Learn to achieve balance (2, again, resonates strongly with 11) between the two sides of your personality and you will achieve great things in whatever field you choose. Fail to achieve that balance and you may struggle to focus in life, suffering from emotional or mental problems. This is a challenging aspect to live with but can be deeply rewarding for both you and those around you.

48/3.

With this number it is hard not to achieve worldly success and, probably, fame. You have an outgoing and affectionate nature which endears people to you, combined with the practicality and determination to succeed, all of which will make your path easy. There is a certain duality in this combination; you may seem quiet and determined on one level, yet fun-loving and outgoing on another. Show business or TV may well be the place for you to thrive. Journalism may also appeal as you have both insight and determination to find answers to your questions. Success may come suddenly to you – at least as far as others are concerned – but you will have worked quietly behind the scenes for many years. Your ability to spot a chance when it comes along is most likely to be the reason for your sudden rise!

49/4.

With humanity, insight, intuition and solid practical skills it's likely you'll go far in life. Always patient, able and willing to see other's point of view, you like to build new and successful relationships wherever you go. Your wide intellectual and emotional skills are well controlled and this means you have a great combination of talents to make you successful in many areas of life – though business leadership may suit you best. Your health, stamina and energy levels are particularly strong and you will enjoy an active life in both sport and business. This is a well-balanced combination which creates an opportunity for growth and development in both spiritual and practical ways. Your ability to theorize is extremely strong but can, on occasion, lead you focus on theory rather than on practicality.

50/5.

With this combination you'll be surrounded by people, friends, family and acquaintances; and you'll just love it.

Emotional richness, intuitive insight and a constant curiosity about those around you will make you the perfect friend, lover or partner. Life will be full of movement for you; this can be in frequent changes of scene or simply in a lot of invites to events and parties. Your inquisitive nature tends to lead you to a scientific career and your creativity and imagination will give you strong abilities in this field. You will be a pioneer, thanks to your vision, and have the eloquence to make yourself heard. Fame may come your way but you would prefer to have fun and make new discoveries! Natural, relaxed and happy when learning, you will be much sought after in every area of your life.

51/6.

Inquisitive, inspired and protective; you have many qualities that make a great warrior and leader. Leadership for you may mean going into battle rather than directing government. This can be taken in either a literal sense or a more metaphorical one. You lead causes, be they social ones or political ones, with equal valor and determination. Your talents make you ideal for legal careers, military or police roles. Your mind will be restless and you will seek new inspiration frequently. Your strength appears as a calm, outward appearance although you may be experiencing all manner of turmoil inside! This control is a great skill and asset and is likely to be one of the main reasons you find yourself at the front of the charge, whatever the battle.

52/7.

This number brings together an inquisitive nature, with a need for balance and great, humanitarian and insightful nature. You explore the world around you in great detail, including the people you encounter. You assess, balance and develop a natural understanding of what you see. In general you will have sought educational opportunities early in life but if these have been unavailable you will make up for that at a later date. You take well to education and it is a crucial part of your life, which means teaching is a good career for you. You have a level of understanding that runs much deeper that most people can comprehend and this can lead you to isolation. Those with this combination may prefer to live alone, in some isolation, but will need to find an outlet for their thirst for knowledge. Balance is a key part of this number and finding balance in the self will allow you to find peace and harmony in any circumstances and amidst the many changes you may face in life.

53/8.

This number can seem aggressive, tyrannical and domineering. In fact it demonstrates a sure self-knowledge that you can accomplish any task laid before you. Self-assurance is a key part of this combination. Your intellect rules your emotions – hence the appearance of a dominating personality. You have both strong intellect and high ambition which means a career in the law may appeal. You love sifting fact from fiction and you love applying this technique to people as much as abstract concepts. Again, this can lead you towards the legal profession or to work as a detective. Your method of defense is to attack, as a result of your ability to examine information or people you are often first to spot a threat or potential one. Your ultimate aim though is defend yourself, or those under your protection, and although your aggressive side comes to the fore often it is used largely to defend others' interests.

54/9.

Combining wit with charm and intelligence you are self-possessed and popular. There is a practical side to your intelligence and you work well with your hands at building or creating. Technology may fascinate you and it could be in this field that your sharp mind will be at its happiest. There is a deep routed restlessness in your soul but this is a restlessness in the search of both knowledge and humanitarian goals. The latter can give you the focus you need to remain committed to a project and if technology can be used to find practical solutions to a problem facing a group of people you'll be in your element. You have a personality that can seem conventional to others and you are interested in the past and in established institutions. Your ultimate goal is, however, to create change that will benefit the wider world and you may become something of a "fifth-columnist" should you perceive that these venerable institutions require changing! If this is the case, that change will happen.

55/1.

Inquisitive, inquiring and motivated by change, driven by the latter in fact, you can be a difficult person on occasion. This combination of numbers does, however, bring the qualities needed to be an inspirational leader. You have no trouble in expressing your opinions and these opinions are naturally unique and original. Your desire to know and your natural abilities at searching for information make it possible for you to discover secrets or information overlooked by others. You can create whole new perspectives on any situation and may use this to your own advantage. Above all you are productive – driven by the need to create. The homes of those people governed by this number are often filled with many children! You have an acute sense of justice which you are capable of dispensing quickly and sharply but your sense of fairness tempers this towards a merciful outcome.

56/11.

Again, an expression of the Master Number 11. With a strong desire to create a peaceful, safe world you combine intuition with a sharp intelligence. You have a high energy level and the expression of 5 in this combination focuses your energy on constant activity. You work tirelessly towards your vision. This nature can be a difficult one for others to be around but you have a natural charm and skill at negotiation. You are loyal to your family and/or to any cause to which you are committed. Once you have made a commitment you will see it through to the end and your inexhaustible energy will nearly always see the outcome you desire. However, and this can seem contradictory to others on occasion, you have strong abilities at seeing the other side of an argument. Your analytical skills may lead you to change your mind, believing that the right outcome is not the one you initially thought. This sudden switch can be a shock for those who do not have your flexibility.

57/3.

You have a natural ability to understand others and spend much time in doing so. Deeply charitable, you will not only understand but help when required. Your ability to give so freely can be taken advantage of and this can lead you to feel negative and self-pitying. Learning to laugh at yourself will help! Your moods are extremely changeable; the emotional depth brought here by the 7 is subject to the need for change of the 5. Your inner life is where your need for change is fed and this can be disconcerting to others. Learning to express your emotions through the arts is a good way to manage this complexity in your personality and will stimulate you and help others to understand both you and themselves. You are a strong humanitarian with a need to see progress in the world and will work to achieve this in big and small ways throughout your life. Sometimes, although you are always available for others, you find difficulty in finding those willing to support you and this can lead to a profound sense of loneliness which should be combated through actively finding ways to express yourself.

58/4.

Skilled and practical your personality is honest and open. Discipline and tradition may be very important to you and you are an individual with a deep sense of fairness and justice. You explore the detail of any situation or relationship, learn quickly from your findings and then find a practical way in which to use them. There is a high level of mental activity innate in this vibration. While popular with many people, you have a strong need for being on your own; your mind needs time to analyze and find solutions. Your life will have a solid grounding and yet, from time to time, you'll feel the need for change and stimulation. Travel is a good way to feed this need and to also find new projects to entertain your mind. While the need for different scenery is strong, you'll also find that at the end of a journey you will be glad to be home - back to the mundane practicalities of daily life.

59/5.

A life influenced by this number will be full of travel, change, challenges and excitement; which is exactly what you need to thrive. You have a natural ability to see the big picture, to see the needs of those around you and to evaluate risks. This number can be that of a gambler, one who has great insight and likes to take risks. In the business world those working in the financial markets or speculative investments may well find that they have this number influencing their lives. With an exceptionally quick mind and many choices in life it's important, however, to guard against impulsiveness. The personality represented by this number is talkative, influential and adaptable. You do have a strong sense of idealism and may seek leadership roles where you can help to build a better world or foster improvement. This life will be a busy one but will be an effective one for positive change.

60/6.

Those under the vibration of this number will find that they must work hard to make a living and to build success in life. They have the possibility to make a strong, secure future for themselves but this future will take time to manifest.

Achievement here is the result of hard work. Something of an enigma, these people will prefer to work alone, yet need a close, strong family. Idealist in many senses, your need for perfection and completion can seem obsessive. There is however great power with this vibration and the ability to make a success in any field. The naturally protective nature of the 6, protective and nurturing, may make for the ideal nurse or carer. There are also great artistic possibilities within this number but, again, success is the result of hard work in this field and may take many years to achieve.

61/7.

With a calm and deliberate assurance you can achieve great control over others with this number in your chart. You seek perfection and completion, will use sheer personal strength to achieve it and have patience to see any project through. You have a strong interest in the esoteric and the spiritual. In this case the 6, which can express home, may relate to a community of individuals. You may seek to preach, teach and inspire. The religious or spiritual life has a strong appeal for you and it is one for which you are well suited. You have a strong sense of ethics in your own life and are keen to foster this in others. If you do not join a religious or spiritual group it is likely you will seek to serve the wider community in other ways – diplomacy or government administration are fields where you may feel a calling. Although you have the ability to control others you are not self-serving; this is a deeply altruistic vibration and you will always be called to serve on some level.

62/8.

Safety, security and harmony are important to you if this number is one of your personal numbers. Through these routes you will find power, wisdom and influence. In whatever field you choose you will find mastery but first you must learn to master yourself. You have a deeply analytical mind and will spend much time analyzing yourself, particularly when you are younger. The level of understanding that this teaches you will help to build strong relationships with others. You can be protective or over-protective, and you must guard against this. Your natural and developed authority can also be domineering. Focus your efforts on helping others to achieve balance and build security in their own lives and you will find much success in your own.

63/9.

The world's sorrows are your concern and you will set out early in life to address these. You seek reform and justice – not for yourself but for others. This is a very balanced vibration in which the heart and the head work together to make *everything* better. There is a strongly self-sacrificing trait amongst people who are influenced by this number.

They may have a secure and safe home and loving family which they may lose in order to pursue a greater happiness for others. With strong artistic traits and intuitive skills you are determined to create and to help; this can be a lonely path and one that may seem selfish to your closest family. You may choose paths that take you away from everything you hold dear and yet do so in the knowledge that you are benefiting them too in the end. You battle against the odds in life and this is truly inspirational. Spending time around much sorrow and strife can take its toll and you should be careful to guard against this.

64/1.

Deeply individualistic and highly popular this is a strange number! You'll work hard to build security and have all the practical skills to do so, along with plenty of unique ways of achieving it. Yet your focus may not be home and family but a group of friends or associates. Friendship is often the most valuable thing for you – money and possessions will take second place. It's the security of people that you seek, not wealth. You have a natural work ethic and will work hard at whatever you choose to do. A natural judge of people you make good choices when it comes to your close circle. You may not have many close friendships (though many acquaintances) but those that are closest will be deep and life-long friendships. Your intuition, insight and individual approach to life will almost certainly lead you to a creative life; the arts will be where you find your outlet. Again, money, fame and success will be less important than achieving perfection. When you start a project you'll see it through, however long, hard or unpleasant it is.

65/11.

In this case the Master Number 11 promises worldly success and achievement. Methodical, careful, intelligent and mature you persevere to carve out security in the world. You will rarely do this alone, always valuing the input of those around you. You may seem reserved to some at first but you like to build relationships slowly and carefully to ensure that the are sound. You rise may be slow and steady but you will find an uncanny ability to meet people of influence will be part of the benefits of this number. Your natural politeness and interest in others will ensure you are noted by these people. Generally, thanks to taking time to building strong relationships, you will make a good, lasting marriage or partnership. Divorce is not usually a feature of your life as you are prepared to work at everything in your life.

66/3.

Responsible, wise and with a strong sense of public welfare you may find that idealism rules your life. You strive for perfection and will work hard to achieve it. You have a natural charisma which draws to you the people and things you need to make your dreams reality. By building a strong base and material wealth you find a great deal of satisfaction in life but you will need to share your fortune to be truly satisfied. Charity work is a must for you. A strong and secure home means a strong and secure community as far as you are concerned and the welfare of others is a natural priority for you. Intrinsically you have a strong understanding of value – the result being that you make good investments throughout your life. The home, community and life you build will be a good one and you will live to see the fruits of your labors enjoyed by many.

67/4.

Mature and trustworthy you are likely to take a practical approach to life. You value material progress in life and have a unique combination of skills and abilities which make you well placed to achieve success in this part of your life. 6 craves the security of home and strives to protect this but combined with 7 this urge is focused in a wider sense towards the community in general. The vibration of 4 contributes to your efforts common sense and practical skills to achieve all of this. You will use your talents creatively and artistically to build real, solid achievements which benefit the wider community. Home and family will always be important to you but this is a home that you will be happy to share with others. Sociable, intelligent and outgoing your home will be the center of many lives within your wider circle. You seem to emanate solidity, practicality and creativity which will draw many people into your life.

68/5.

With a love of luxury and security you will work hard to achieve both. Valuing knowledge is a strong influence with the vibrations of this combination. You will have strong research skills which you use to accumulate both knowledge and wealth. The outer trappings of wealth and power are important to you and you may risk obsessing over these. 68 can mean that you may seem introverted but you are a good communicator when you wish to be. You also enjoy listening to other people, constantly seeking stimulation, information and new ideas. Planning is one of your strongest attributes and you gather information carefully, organize it and then plan on the basis of your findings. Administrative careers are ideal but you will most likely achieve a position of authority in whatever field you choose. This is partly due to the calm air of confidence and your clear abilities at successfully completing projects.

69/6.

This number has strong material elements. It represents building material success in the world. Projects, once undertaken, will be seen through to fruition with patience, energy and competence. You will find that resources come readily to hand but must focus on making the most of these resources. Luxury and wealth are important to you and must fill your life with significant resources before you feel comfortable and able to express yourself fully. Often reserved, you will however attract many people into your life – you may see these people as resources. Once you have achieved your success it is in your nature to share it. It's likely that people with this combination will work in the world of business or finance but when they have achieved their goals their wealth will be used to benefit the arts or social projects. You wish your love of beauty to be shared and you understand that material wealth is only important on the earthly plane – wishing it to benefit as many people as possible.

70/7.

This is another combination that is likely to take you into the world of business. Creative and intelligent, you believe in both fairness and opportunity and work well in business partnerships. You display a natural tendency towards thriftiness in both your home and working life, which will help you to achieve the financial rewards you seek. There is a practicality to this vibration which means you will create solid foundations for success in your life. Challenges and changes come with this vibration but you are adept mentally at adjusting to new situations and actually thrive on the challenge. This ease of adjustment also means that travel is likely to feature in your life and you have strong talents for learning languages and adapting to new customs. If your working life takes you to many different countries or involves travel in any way, it's likely that you will thrive.

71/8.

Individual, intelligent and driven by ambition. This number is a dynamic, energetic expression of the number 8. You are never distracted by the accepted way of doing things – though you will act traditionally if you perceive it as the best way to get ahead. The natural intelligence and individuality that this number bestows means that your rise to success can be rapid. It is however based on real skills and you will be seen as dependable, inspirational and able. This number has masses of energy and drive; this can lead to exhaustion and lack of enthusiasm if you don't remember to take time off. Your natural individuality makes you very creative but to preserve this creativity you must take time to re-charge, once in a while. In your personal life you will be loving and affectionate but must find a partner who can keep up with your seemingly unstoppable pace!

72/9.

Analytical and with great powers of deduction, you are well placed to manage financial affairs. Material advantage is important to you and are able to manage money prudently and cleverly. Balancing acts are the way in which you avoid wastefulness, ensuring that all of your assets are carefully aligned to create the best advantage for you. It is important to you for your life to be constructive, you dislike being inactive though must remember that even "down-time" has its purposes. You express yourself well and have a character that is strong and stable. While you are keenly materially focused you have a strong empathy with others and will work for their benefit as well. You dislike waste – and wasted talent is your biggest dislike so you will have a strong desire to develop it in those around you. Although a good number for those pursuing business careers it's also a strong vibration for teaching and mentoring.

73/1.

This number has a great deal of promise in the business and financial world but while you will often achieve success in this field you are aware that this is simply not enough. Having a strong, affectionate and patient nature you understand that your deeper self needs more than material success to create stability. While you focus creatively on creating wealth, you rarely do so to benefit yourself but look to make the world a better place for all. You can endure hardship and have great stamina and you will use these qualities to create successful outcomes in all of your projects. Most of these will focus on building wealth (material and spiritual) for those around you. You have a strong link to your higher self and you appreciate that its welfare is as important as your physical comfort. Stable, well-rounded and communicative you will have a lasting impact on those around you.

74/11.

The final occurrence of the Master Number 11 combines intellect with practicality. This number can lead to a career in science – most likely in chemistry, medical or biological sciences. You believe in making the world "right" and will set about to achieve this end through the application of practical skills and science in some form or other. Independent, charming and with considerable poise, you are well liked by all around you. You have a gentle ease with people which makes you popular. With a high level of individuality and practicality in this vibration you will approach problems in new ways but with the means to resolve them. You don't suffer fools gladly and like to create real solutions to real problems. Success is likely with this combination and material gains highly likely. You will naturally seek to share these gifts with others and will be keen to see that the fruits of your labor benefit others.

75/3.

You will need persistence and patience with this combination of numbers. You have strong inner resources, which will help, but must remain consistently independent to achieve success. Luckily you understand that your efforts will bring success but may find that your slow progress makes others doubt your chances. However, self-discipline, inner strength and self-confidence all will bring success in the end. This can be a long road and one filled with unexpected challenges, changes and set backs. But in the end you will triumph. You have an outgoing nature that will make you popular and you thrive when you are on show. Performance is important to you and you may find your career in any field in which you demonstrate your skills to the public. Your intelligence and intuition can mean that this may be in a theatrical setting but your physical endurance may lead you to sports. This is the number of a dancer, an athlete or a boxer! Wide experience in life will lead you to a great wisdom and your insight into people will be invaluable in your progress.

76/4.

Behind this number lies the power of genius. With wisdom, insight and intellect all poised towards achieving completion, you also have practicality rooted in your soul. Working alone will appeal and you are painstaking in your approach. Engineering, craftsmanship and quality are all important to you and you may work in a trade or craft where precision and skill is crucial. While this number can lead to great material success this is not where you find fulfillment, a job well done is what drives you. What you create will benefit you in many ways and will be even more beneficial to the wider world. Although you have the ability to create wealth it's likely that you will see this as a means to creating yet more and better things. Your personal needs are fairly basic and you will often live a simple lifestyle. Highly popular, you will also be keen to create relationships that "work" - you can obsess over this to the point of driving people away, if you are not careful. However, your commitment is so deep it will be appreciated by many.

77/5.

Insight is one of the key attributes of this number and insight into people is a strong feature. You enjoy the company of a wide social circle and may work in psychiatry or counseling to feed your need for constant new insights into new people. Analytical and with a wide experience in life, you are able to quickly identify what makes people "tick". You are not above using this to your own advantage but have a natural charm and grace which means this is rarely resented. Material gains in life seem to come from unexpected sources and often you'll find yourself furnished with the means to enjoy life with surprisingly little effort. You have a quiet elegance about you and a sparkle which makes you naturally attractive. People are drawn to you and it's likely you'll have the means to entertain lavishly. Your need for change and variety in life can be overwhelming at times but you can satisfy this with new intellectual projects as well as travel or socializing. If they combine all three you'll be a very happy individual indeed!

78/6.

Adding together the numbers 1 – 12 brings you to 78. This represents both the 12 months of the year and the 12 signs of the Zodiac. This is the number of attainment, achievement, perfection and peace. This is a number that represents all of these and also suggests wisdom, inner peace, accomplishment and completion. You may work hard to achieve all of these aspects but once you have done so the balance in your inner self and the balance in your life are complete. This number suggests a settled, mature individual who has wealth, comfort and a desire to share these gifts. You can offer both emotional or financial support to those in need – be they family or institutions. You are a philosophical soul who has achieved an inner state of balance and can help others towards this goal. This is a number that represents attainment, comfort and philanthropy. Your spiritual side will be important to you but you may not express this in a traditional way. Rounded and confident you will be the focus of many people's affection – affection which you return willingly and generously.

Conclusion

Thank you again for reading this book!

I hope this book was able to teach how to simply calculate your Personal Numbers and understand the basic and detailed meanings of their vibrations.

The next step is to move on to your friends, family and acquaintances!

Finally, if you enjoyed this book, please take the time to share your thoughts and post a review on Amazon. It'd be greatly appreciated!

Thank you and good luck!

CRYSTALS

ULTIMATE LIST OF CRYSTALS AND THEIR USES, CRYSTAL HEALING AND ENERGY FIELDS

Written By

Mia Rose

Introduction

I want to thank you and congratulate you for getting the book, *"Crystals, The Ultimate Guide to Crystal Healing"*.

This book contains proven steps and strategies on how to use crystals to heal both physical and mental conditions along with techniques to care for crystals, choose crystals and the benefits of different types of precious and semi-precious stones.

Thanks again for getting this book, I hope you enjoy it!

Chapter 1: Clear as Crystal; Crystal Healing Facts

If you are reading this book on an electronic device (e-book reader, computer, smart-phone) then you're already utilizing the power of crystals. Even if you're reading it in a more physical form the process by which a print copy has been produced will have involved some form of technology in which crystals played a part!

While using crystals within a technological setting may be a standard part of our lives – even if we are not aware of just how many of our existing technological advancements depend on them – some people find it a more difficult concept to understand that crystals can do more than store information or be used to transmit or create electricity.

In fact, crystal healing has long been practiced in many traditional settings – particularly in religious and healing traditions in India and the Far East. In the last century this practice has become more widely established in the west and is now accepted by many as an integral part of many healing traditions.

How Does Crystal Healing Work?

Energy is a force that resonates and radiates throughout everything in the universe. Without energy nothing could exist and our own bodies are vibrant with this essential life force. Ill-health is, in part, a manifestation of imbalances within the natural energy field that operates around us. Where these imbalances occur it is possible to use different kinds of energy to re-balance them. Hunger can be dissipated with the energy in our food and cancerous tumors can be dissipated by the energy from radiation (radiotherapy). Everything around us also emanates energy and crystals are unique in that the energy that radiates from them is stable and remains constant. Crystals are formed in patterns and structures which can be used to re-balance or re-tune our own energy fields.

While it is important to take professional medical advice if you suffer from any condition, throughout the ages, crystals have been used to heal and to maintain the balance of our own energy field. The raw energy contained in crystals is easy to attune to; it is formed from the same essential patterns that create all life in the universe. In crystal healing, specific qualities of different crystal structures are used to tune our own energy fields to their correct frequency. As with radiation (which is just light, after all) crystals can radiate energy that can help us to heal and also provide protection from ill-health.

Finding Your Crystals

Crystals have different qualities and even individual crystals of the same type will resonate differently on a very subtle level. Finding the right crystals for you is actually very easy – in fact the crystals will be more likely to find you! Simply holding a crystal in your hand will, with some practice, identify if it's the right crystal for you. In reality all crystals have beneficial qualities and as you start to work with crystals your choices can be more specific. Attuning yourself to crystals can take time – though for some individuals it is a faster process than for others. In this book we'll take you through some simple steps which will help on your journey including a close look at how to care for crystals and meditations to use when working with them.

If you have a very specific issue which you wish to address with crystals then finding an appropriate crystal which has links to that condition will be useful. However, intuition plays a large part in crystal healing and simply holding a crystal in your hand can often indicate if it is the right crystal for you. In this book we'll also take a look at some of the most popular crystals and their uses but always look to your reaction to a crystal to decide whether it can benefit you in anyway.

Crystals and the Chakras

Crystal healing is strongly associated with the concept of Chakras. These are traditional "energy" points identified in a number of healing systems, particularly those with roots in India and the Far East. The Chakras are understood as spinning, energy vortexes where our own individual energy field connects to the wider universe and to the greater energy that flows through it. Crystals are used for their own very strong qualities at focusing this energy to direct it into relevant energy points within the body and they can balance or stimulate the individual Chakras. For those new to energy healing, the recipe for success is simple; to address specific issues identify the Chakra that controls the particular bodily functions (or emotions) with which there is a problem and then use the crystals associated with the same conditions or energy. The seven primary Chakras are as follows;

1. The Base Chakra, or the Root Chakra is located at the base of the spine. This is related to physicality, grounding and a sense of belonging. It is associated with the color red and with our basic physical needs such as food and shelter.

2. Colored Orange, the Sacral Chakra is located a couple of inches below the navel and is linked to our relations with others, including romantic and sexual relationships. This Chakra is related to emotional issues, sexuality and our ability to experience pleasure.

3. The Solar Plexus Chakra, colored yellow is located in the upper portion of the abdomen around the stomach. This chakra relates to our sense of self, to confidence and our ability to be open and honest.

4. The Heart Chakra, colored green, is located in the center of our chest around the heart itself. It relates to our ability to love in the wider sense, our sense of respect for those around us and our ability to give of ourselves. The chakra governs health issues related to stress and to physical issues related to both the heart and lungs.

5. The Throat Chakra, colored blue, is located around our throats! It is related to communication, expression and creativity. Physically it can relate to throat and breathing issues, colds and flu.

6. The Third Eye Chakra, colored indigo, is located between the eyes on the forehead. This chakra is linked to wisdom, intuition and to decision making. It is related to mental issues and anxiety disorders including a range of depressive illnesses.

7. The Crown Chakra; this chakra is colored violet (although considered to be colorless by some). It is located at the very top of our head. This chakra is related to spirituality, to bliss and to a connection with the wider universal forces. Illnesses including Alzheimer's, headaches, dizziness, depression and

more serious mental illnesses such as schizophrenia are linked with this chakra.

Colors and Crystals

Colors have strong magical and healing associations in their own right and can be found playing a role in many different magical traditions from candle magic to chakra healing. The basic associations with each color are relevant in crystal healing as well, and these are described below:

- Red; signifies both fire and blood and is associated with both anger and focus. Passion, action and purification are also strongly associated with the color. Achieving grace through purification is also strongly linked to this color and it has powerful associations with radical change and healing.

- Orange; this color indicates spirituality, bravery, inspirational spontaneity, sociability, intelligence and contentment. Achieving balance and harmony in life is a strong feature of the associations with this color and it can be beneficial at establishing a sense of contentment.

- Yellow; a very individual color, yellow signifies creativity, focus, inspiration, ingenuity and inventiveness. It is associated with the sun, for obvious reasons, and was the imperial color in China where garments of yellow were worn by the Emperor alone. It is associated strongly with authority, power and strength.

- Green; this color has many complex associations and it's the color that we see all around us. It symbolizes the earth, fertility and, in many cultures, has strong associations with the concept of the divine. Benevolence, temperance and empathy are common associations with this color and it is also strongly associated with good luck.

- Blue; the color of the heavens and the oceans, blue represent tranquility, peace, rest, recovery and good health. Associations with the sky mean that it linked to the element of air and to clarity of thought, while associations with oceans link it to emotions and particularly to serenity and peace.

- Indigo; a deeper form of blue, this color is associated with many similar attributes to that of blue but on a deeper level. Deep intellectual thought, serenity and peace of mind on the deepest level are all associations that come with this color. Wisdom and intuition are both strongly associated with indigo, as is the concept of justice.

- Violet; abundance, good fortune, plenty and leadership qualities are often associated with this color. In the west it was the color of emperors (as with yellow in the east) and many perceive this color to have similar connotations for this reason. Wealth and power are often associated with violet.

- White; a complex color that is associated with both clarity and purity but also with coldness and distance. White is, in fact, the absence of color and has associations with completion, the beginning and ends of cycles in all areas of life. It is the color of virginity, or youth, yet it is also the color of mourning, in many cultures, signifying death, old age and loss.

- Black; like white, this is another complex color with many associations. Again, used in mourning, it can also be associated with strength, prudence, wisdom and loyalty. Black is also the color of night and this creates associations with both magic and dreams along with intuitive knowledge and hidden knowledge.

Crystal Care and Cleaning

Crystals vibrate with energy and they can also store energy from all around them. They are not discriminating when it comes to absorbing vibrations and will pick up both positive and negative energies from the environment in which they are placed. For this reason it's important to take good care of your crystals and to ensure that they remain filled with positive, healing energy. Cleansing a crystal and "programming" it is a simple process and can be done in a number of ways. The two most common ways use water to help clean away negative vibrations. Some practitioners recommend using spring water (which is ideal) but a basic cleanse can be completed using running water of any kind (including from a tap!). Below are three common methods used to cleanse crystals.

1. Hold your stone under a source of running water; this can be a stream or tap, or water poured from a bottle or jug. Only use cold or slightly warm water, never hot. As the water flows over the stone simply visualize the negative energy and vibrations flowing away from the crystal and pure, positive energies flowing from your body into the stone. Do not dry using a towel or cloth but leave to dry naturally in the sun.

2. Place a bowl of water on a windowsill and add sea-salt giving it a good stir to ensure the salt is dissolved. Place your crystal in the bowl making sure that it is completely covered with water. Ideally do this at the start of the day as the sun rises and leave until midday when the sun is at its full height. Then remove the crystal and dry in the sunlight, as mentioned in the first method.

3. For quartz crystals, in particular, simply burying them in the earth is recommended by many practitioners. The planet itself is made up of approximately one third quartz and the magnetic energy fields that this creates will help to cleanse your crystals in the most natural way. This both cleans and energizes your crystals. This

method can be used for any crystal but is most effective for quartz of all kinds.

Programming Crystals

Crystal healing and meditation works by using the crystal's ability to store and focus energy. Crystals naturally pick up vibrations from around them but by programming your crystals you can focus the crystal's energy on a particular purpose. Once you have programmed a particular crystal the programming will remain and the energy that the crystal emits will continue to provide focus on the matter in question. If you wish, you can "clear" this programming and/or "reprogram" the crystal as desired. Stones can be used for any purpose, for healing or protection, for luck, for love or for financial gain.

As each type of precious or semi-precious stone has different associations you should choose the most appropriate stone for your specific goal. Before you program a stone, or stones, you must be careful to clearly define your goal and the purpose for which you wish the stone to work. Properly programmed a crystal will be focused and powerful but clarity is crucial; remember that the stone cannot "think" for itself, if you are not sure of your own intention then this uncertainty will be fed into the stone!

To focus your thoughts simply think through what you require from the stone and write down this intention in a single sentence. Keep the sentence as short as possible with only one main point. Once you have this thought clearly in your mind you can begin to program your crystal.

Simply sit in a quiet space where you will not be interrupted and hold the stone in your hand (use your left hand if you are left handed or right if right handed). Some people like to burn an incense associated with the same purpose with which they wish to program the stone but, at first, it may be better to limit the distractions around you.

Focus on the stone, study it and feel its weight in your hand. Allow yourself to sense its energy, vibration and power. Gradually you will begin to feel a sense of harmony with the stone as it attunes to your energy and you to its. At this point the stone is ready to be programmed.

Deepen your focus on the stone and say out loud what purpose you wish the stone to fulfill. You can use your written statement if you wish and repeat this several times as you continue to focus on the crystal in your palm. Remain sitting quietly for a moment or two, still focused on the crystal and the thought with which you are programming it. Feel the energy in the crystal pulsing in your hand and imagine the outcome that you wish to achieve.

Once the stone is programmed it will retain the energy you have placed into it. You may wish to place the stone under your pillow or either carry it with you or place it in a specific location in your home. Crystals can pass their energy into other crystals if they touch, so you may wish to wrap the crystal in plain cloth to ensure that messages, energies and intentions don't become mixed. If this does happen by accident you'll need to cleanse your stones as described above and then reprogram them.

Chapter 2: Basic Meditation Techniques

Meditation is an ancient technique found in nearly every religious tradition – big or small – and in every culture throughout history. It can remove stress, create calm and is recognized as a treatment for depression, anxiety and many related disorders by doctors and the medical establishments in many different countries. The full health benefits of meditation have not been fully researched but medical experts agree that it can not only help with mental health but be beneficial for many physical conditions and is even a natural pain killer!

Meditating with crystals is the perfect way to not only program the crystals themselves but also to focus your own mind on a specific goal. Depending on your intentions or needs, you should choose an appropriate crystal for the meditation (see the section on types of crystals later in this book). In this chapter we'll take a look at basic meditations that can be used as a framework to meditate with crystals and can be adapted for different purposes.

Meditation Basics

Always meditate in a quiet space, where you will not be interrupted. Some people choose to meditate with candles, incense or music and all of these can be helpful in achieving a state of relaxation. Choose which, if any, works for you and try different methods until you find the most effective "tools".

Wear loose fitting clothing (or none at all) and ensure that the room (or space) is at a comfortable heat. As you meditate your body's processes will slow and you may feel colder.

Remaining physically comfortable is important when meditating; you can meditate for a few moments or much longer, especially as you practice, so minimizing any possible distractions, including physical ones, is essential.

After meditating it can be important to bring yourself firmly back into the real world. Have a hot drink and snack, play some louder music, go for a walk in the fresh air and sunlight (or wind and rain!). Ground yourself back in the real world in whatever way suits you best.

Basic Mindfulness Meditation

Mindfulness is a meditation technique that has roots in Buddhist practice and it is one of the most common meditation techniques used today. Mindfulness meditation can be conducted anywhere, anytime and is a way of simply relaxing and fully experiencing the moment. You can practice mindfulness meditation at home, work or in the park (though be sure to practice relaxation techniques in a safe place). It's a good type of meditation for those learning to meditate and will help you to develop your skills in order to be able to conduct deeper, more effective forms of meditation. The following basic mindfulness meditation can last for as long, or short, a period as you require.

1. Focus your attention on the moment; stand or sit upright and close your eyes.
2. Ask yourself "what am I experiencing right now? What thoughts, what feelings, what physical sensations?"
3. Acknowledge each thought, emotion, sensation, good and bad alike.
4. Gradually redirect your attention to your breathing. Simply focus on the sensation of the air entering your lungs and leaving your lungs. Breath in through your nose and out through your mouth.
5. Allow your sense of awareness to expand once more, to each physical sensation, sounds and your own presence in the space in which you are meditating. Continue to breath regularly and deeply.
6. As thoughts surface, note them and move on. Do not allow one thought to distract you but continue to focus on the present, physical moment.
7. Conclude by stretching, yawning, taking a deep breath in and opening your eyes as you expel the air from your lungs.

Pyramid Meditation

This meditation will help you to learn to visualize – an important part of meditation, healing and crystal healing. Use it to practice and develop both your meditation skills and your crystal healing skills.

1. Hold your crystal in either hand – whichever feels "right" and sit on the floor in a cross legged position.

2. Close your eyes and take three deep breaths, breathing in through the nose and filling the lungs. Hold each breath to the count of three. Expel the air from your lungs in a short breath through your mouth. Repeat this process two more times. You may feel a little light-headed but this is normal.

3. Count backwards from nine to one taking a breath at each number. Do this slowly and rhythmically and as you do so remind yourself to return to full consciousness in ten or fifteen minutes. Your mind and internal body clock should do this automatically but if you prefer you can set an alarm.

4. Continue to breath at the rate you have established in step three and with your eyes closed begin to focus on the color associated with your aims. This should be the same color as the crystal you are using.

5. Visually, in your mind, construct a pyramid, with the tip located a foot or so above your head. The four points should fall on the floor around you, two behind

and two in front. Imagine the color flooding this pyramid.

6. If you are using the meditation for healing, feel the color washing around you within the pyramid and focus it towards the area you wish to heal, or the source of pain.

7. Towards the end of the session, either when your own internal alarm begins to bring you back to fuller consciousness or the alarm you have set rings, simply focus on your breathing and count back from one to nine and open your eyes at nine.

8. Visually imagine the pyramid dissolve around you and focus for a moment or two on the crystal in your hand. Once you feel you have fully returned to consciousness end the meditation and ground yourself back in the real world.

Chapter 3: Crystal Attributes in Detail

All crystals can be used in crystal healing – including precious stones. While you may not wish to start a collection of rubies, diamonds, emeralds or sapphires it's possible that you already have some jewelery that features one or more of them. While loose stones are better for crystal healing purposes you can still focus energy on jewelery pieces and this has the advantage that you can carry the positively charged energy with you as you go! If you do choose to purchase small precious gemstones for use in crystal healing they can be very powerful stones indeed. In this section we'll take a tour of the big four!

Precious Gemstones

Diamonds

The traditional image of diamonds is of the crystal clear variety but diamonds do come in a wide range of colors. If you choose to use diamonds in crystal healing the different colors will have associations of their own. The most common color variations are pink, yellow, blue and black.

Diamonds symbolize clarity and purity; they are strongly associated with love and partnership, bringing clarity and honesty into relationships. In crystal healing they can be used to establish strong, deep bonds in personal relationships, to create fidelity and trust between partners. The gem is also associated with abundance, wealth and great energy. In crystal healing diamonds are particularly powerful at helping to create the atmosphere for accumulation of wealth and success – both of the lasting kind. There is great strength in diamonds and this is one of their key associations, stimulation individuality, creativity and brilliance of mind.

Rubies

These fiery stones are full to the brim with explosive energy! They are associated with passion, change, sensuality and lust. In healing terms they are excellent at dispelling lethargy, at improving both circulation and breathing. They encourage self-expression and innovative thought, so are useful stones to carry when studying or taking exams. The association that these stones have with fire is also in the sense of fires in which all manner of things are forged and this can make them useful stones to use for good luck with creating new things – both physical and intellectual. Invention, innovation and the ability to bring about great change are all encapsulated in the qualities that this gemstone can impart.

Emeralds

Keenly associated with love, luck and fertility, this stone can create a powerful healing affect in all of these areas. It creates an atmosphere of loyalty in close personal relationships and encourages friendship and respect. Strongly associated with the earth, with growth and with sustenance, the green colored emerald is a perfect stone for use in any healing where positive growth and change is required. Emerald is associated with luck too and for anyone needing a little unexpected and surprise assistance in life or love this is the stone to use! Carrying or wearing an emerald offers both protection and guidance and it is often associated with clairvoyance – both the physic ability and also the practical ability to see things as they really are.

Sapphires

Traditionally seen as a deep rich blue, these stones, like diamonds also come in a startling array of colors. Blue, yellow, black, pink, white, green and indigo are all variations on the theme of sapphires. The stone itself is strongly associated with wisdom and imparts a deep knowledge to those who use it. The different shades may address different areas of life and knowledge but all impart a deeply rooted understanding of that area. Sapphire is also known for its ability to create balance and harmony in both the body and mind. It can be a very healing stone which can be used to bring the body back into an equilibrium after an illness or to calm the mind. Bringers of joy and serenity, sapphires are also known for their ability to attract gifts, to make dreams come true and to find fulfillment.

<u>Crystals</u>

Crystals used in healing can be sourced cheaply and easily. Many can be bought online but it's often wise to buy crystals in a real-world store. This give you the opportunity to feel the energy within the crystal and evaluate whether it is the right crystal for you. Sometimes, when searching for new crystals one will "jump" out at you, which is a good sign that you would benefit strongly from the stone. Online stores do, however, offer a great deal of convenience and can be a great way to source new crystals as you become more experienced working with them.

There is a massive range of different types of crystal and finding the right crystals to work with is largely a matter of personal choice and specific needs. In this section we'll take a look at some of the most commonly used crystals that have long been used for healing. A number of crystals come in different forms and in this section we'll look at the uses of different crystals and their sub-forms.

Agates

Agates have a soothing and calming effect and can be used in a great range of healing applications. They come in several different forms each with their own unique qualities and appearance.

- Standard agate is a beautiful stone, with unusual patterns running through it. Agate creates inner strength, poise and a sense of serenity. It works slowly, bringing peace and self-acceptance, making it a good stone for work on emotional issues. All agates are believed to bring analytical abilities and the ability to solve problems in a practical way.

- Crazy-lace, or Mexican Agate, creates confidence and a sense of well being. It relieves emotional pain and stress and will attract positive energies and people into your life. Physically it can foster energy in the major organs and remove energy blockages in the Chakras.

- Fire agate is a very protective stone. An excellent stone to carry with you, it offers a shield against negative thoughts and intentions in others. Fire agate brings a sense of safety, security and strength. Physically it is ideal for healing stomach problems, cravings and helps in the treatment of addictions of all kinds.

- Moss agate comes in a beautifully patterned, subtle green color. As with any green stone it is associated with luck, growth and prosperity. It is a stone of fresh starts and should be worn or programmed to aid with any new project in life. Physically it will help with recovery from injuries, speed recovery from colds and flu and is believed to be good for reducing pain and inflammation.

- Tree agate is a striking white stone with green markings and is closely associated with nature. It helps to create strong structures in life – be they relationships, careers or homes. It is a nurturing stone and offers protection to children, animals and plants. Like a tree, the power in tree agate is slow acting and if used it should be carried for a long time to reap the full benefits.

Amber

Amber is not strictly speaking a crystal! It's the fossilized remains of ancient tree resin and often contains fragments of vegetation or even insects. Although not a crystal as such it's a powerful healing stone and is commonly used in crystal healing. In healing it is believed to be extremely powerful at drawing away negative energy both from physical or emotional sources. Amber soaks away illness and negative emotions and turns them into positive and good health. Physical ailments with which amber can provide relief include stomach disorders, kidney and bladder problems and liver problems.

Amethyst

This beautiful purple stone is highly protective, warding off evil in all its many forms. Traditionally amethyst was believed to ward off nightmares and placing a charged crystal under the pillow or by your bed is recommended. For physical illnesses, amethyst is commonly used to treat headaches, tension and to reduce inflammation (particularly bruising or swelling). Amethyst is also believed to be a powerful stone for combating addictions.

Bloodstone

This is a dark stone with flecks of red running through it and is sometimes known as Heliotrope. It is strongly associated with the blood – with circulation and heart function. It brings grounding and protection and is believed to promote strong friendships. Physically it is used in healing to address liver, kidney and bladder problems, as it aids the removal of toxins from the body. Bloodstone is also believed to have soothing and calming qualities and is commonly placed by the bed to aid natural sleep.

Calcite

Another crystal which comes in a wide range of colors, the general properties of calcite are calming and refreshing.

- Blue calcite is generally light and milky in color, it is restful, peaceful and calming, soothing the body and mind. Physically it is good for lung disorders, breathing related conditions and throat conditions.

- Green calcite is bright, minty, refreshing looking stone. This stone provides strength in difficult situations, mental sharpness and balance. In healing it is used to calm fevers, aid recovery from minor burns and is a good immune system booster.

- Orange calcite is believed to banish negative energy, thoughts and emotions. It is an excellent stone to create positivity in your life and is known to bring energy, laughter and joy into your life. In healing it can be used to treat intestinal disorders and is also commonly used to combat depression by virtue of its positive vibrations.

- Red calcite brings energy in abundance and also promotes optimism. Additionally it also gives the ability to combat fears and remove obstacles in life. Red is associated with the base Chakra and this stone can be effective at treating lower limb disorders and hip problems. It's an excellent all round energizer and can help those with fatigue-related illnesses.

Citrine

Like all crystals colored with a hint of orange this stone promotes positivity. It's great for finding inspiration, tapping into creativity and building self-confidence. The stone is believed to help those wearing it to achieve their goals, particularly personal development goals. It's also believed to attract good luck with money in general. Citrine is a good crystal to help lift depression or anxiety related disorders and physically is a crystal which will promote good health in general and build the immune system.

Fluorite

This crystal is typically banded with different colors. It is believed to assist in the understanding of new ideas and information. Fluorite is a good general healing crystal and is particularly useful at fending off infections, colds or flu. Many healers also ascribe powerful qualities at dealing with inflammation, particularly of the joints, and it's commonly recommended to help those suffering from arthritis.

Garnet

This beautiful red stone resembles the ruby and shares many healing qualities with it's "precious" cousin! This stone protects, energizes and regenerates. Red, often symbolizes life force and, as such, this stone is linked to love and to the sex drive. Historically, associated with the planet Mars, this stone was often found embedded in swords and shields. It offers great power and can be very protective against negativity of all kinds. In healing it is an excellent stone to bring back vitality and confidence and can be particularly useful to those suffering from depression, anxiety or fatigue related illnesses. For anybody dealing with obstacles or facing a "battle" in life, this is the stone to carry or wear.

Hematite

This metallic looking crystal is dark, usually black in color, but has an attractive, silvery sheen to it. This is a truly earthy crystal, being a mineral form of iron oxide. It brings both grounding and inspiration – helping you to think creatively and at the same time keeping your feet firmly planted on the earth. This is a powerful combination and can help to ensure success in any new project. In healing its main properties are helping to restore healthy balance to the blood – being particularly useful for those with anemia. It is also recommended for dealing with problems in the legs – fractures, cramps or foot problems of any kind.

Jade

Long considered sacred, holy and linked to Imperial power in China and the Far East, Jade is a term actually applied to two different crystals; Jadeite and Nephrite. The latter is easier and cheaper to obtain and is a darker, opaque crystal. Jade is imbued with qualities that include promoting independence, strength, courage, wisdom and justice. It is also believed to banish negative thoughts and calm troubled souls. Highly protective, it shares qualities of a luck bringer and fruitful endeavors with many other green stones. For healing it is particularly prized as a balancer of the nervous system and in traditional lore it is used as an aid for fertility and for child-birth.

Jasper

This crystal comes in many and varied forms and colors. All share nurturing and calming qualities and promote strength and tenacity. The energy of the crystal is slow to work and when programing it time should be taken to optimize its potential. For healing purposes carrying jasper, or keeping it close to you, will have the best results.

- Brecciated (Brecceated or Bracciated) Jasper; this stone contains small quantities of Hematite and as such shares grounding qualities. It focuses thought and encourages action; in healing it is used to promote happiness and is useful at combating depression or anxiety.
- Dalmatian Jasper; nurturing and promoting positivity this variety of the stone is commonly used in healing

mental and emotional issues. It is also believed to help boost the immune system and clear toxins from the body.

- Red Jasper; combining the nurturing nature of jasper with the combative nature of all red stones, this crystal is said to promote problem solving. Red jasper brings problems to the fore, in order for them to be dealt with quickly. Clearing blockages is a key attribute and providing grounding and a sense of wellbeing are also ascribed to the stone.

- Yellow Jasper; this is a protective stone and an inspirational one. Traditionally believed to provide protection for travelers it is commonly held to be an antidote to travel and motion sickness. In healing this stone is used to release toxins, aid digestion and improve energy levels. Like all Jaspers, this stone works slowly and should be kept close for best effects.

Lapis Lazuli

This is a deep, rich, blue-colored crystal that has been highly prized as a gem throughout history. It is associated with thought and expression, clarity and intellect. Blue has many associations with the skies (or heavens) and the oceans. Both have an intangible element to them, representing spirituality and depth of emotion. This gem can be used to promote self-knowledge and spiritual awareness. In healing it is commonly used to stabilize blood pressure and to alleviate headaches, migraines and to aid with healthy sleep.

Moldavite

The super-crystal of the healing world, moldavite is rare and is believed to have formed when a meteorite crashed to earth some 15 million years ago. This created a localized deposit of glass-like material with a bottle-green color. The energy in moldavite is tangible and is often experienced as a tingling, hot sensation when the crystal is held. Its healing powers are said to include instilling huge amounts of energy and it's also believed to promote psychic powers. For those new to crystal work it is wise to meditate with a grounding, stone such as Hematite, and a crystal that protects, such as garnet, when first working with moldavite.

Moonstone

As the name would suggest this delicate, milky stone is linked closely to the moon! Traditionally this makes it the stone of women, and it's used for helping reduce PMT. It's also recommended for women as they experience the menopause and is believed to create a sense of calm. Links with the moon also include moonstone in the list of stones connected to luck in fertility and childbirth. In healing moonstone is recommended for many stress related conditions including stomach disorders related to emotional stress. The stone is gentle, working with the user to promote healing.

Obsidian

Formed from rapidly cooled volcanic lava, Obsidian comes in a range of colors thanks to the action of different minerals during its formation. The stones are extremely powerful and not everybody is comfortable working with the stone at first. All obsidians are protective but they work very quickly which can, on occasion, be unsettling!

- Black; although protective this stone can bring negative thoughts and emotions to the fore very quickly. It acts in this way to help remove them, but the experience can be painful. To protect against negative energies, black obsidian is, however, very powerful. It will absorb negativity rapidly and should be cleansed regularly. In healing it aids digestion, cramps and joint and muscular strains, including rheumatism and arthritis.

- Gold; this provides protection and clarity and is an excellent problem solving stone. Again, it is likely to bring a problem right to your door in order for you to deal with it! In healing it is recommended for balancing the energy field in the body and is a good general healing stone.

- Silver; this form of obsidian resembles hematite to some extent with a subtle silvery sheen. It is, again, a powerful protector and is generally used to help in meditation, as it is believed to calm and ground at the same time.

- Snow-flake; lightly patterned with white "snowflakes" this obsidian is ideal at protecting from negativity and, particularly, grief. It helps to heal gently, after loss, and will promote positive thinking. In healing this is a stone that is widely used to help with skin conditions and is believed to aid with clearing the complexion.

Peridot

This charming, light green crystal is a powerful healing and cleansing stone. It, like any green stone, is linked to healthy, abundant growth, good luck, fortune and protection. It is also associated with helping to deal with guilt, obsession and addiction. It creates a quiet, calm sense of confidence in the user and promotes self-confidence and honesty. In healing it is strongly linked with matters of the heart, both emotionally and physically.

Quartz

This is probably the best known of all healing crystals and also comes in a range of colors and varieties. It contains all the spectrum of light and, for this reason, is known for its power as a general, heal-all crystal. It will create positivity and will amplify the positive in life. In addition, it can create active problem solving, provide clarity and banish negative thoughts from your mind, also banishing negativity from other people around you. Quartz brings the ability to be incisive, act quickly and with confidence.

- Rose; light, pink and translucent this form of quartz is associated with love, beauty and trust. It promotes positive emotions, banishes jealousy or resentment. In healing it is used to help skin problems (including the ability to soothe burns or blisters), clear the complexion and is also used to deal with heart problems and lung problems.

- Rutilated; this quartz has spikes of golden brown color embedded deep within its structure. The stone is believed to promote vitality, energy and to banish depression. In healing it is used to combat phobias and fears and is strongly linked with healing depression. Its ability to rejuvenate is believed to help with healing exhaustion (physical and mental) and is a useful stone for athletes.

- Smoky quartz has similar attributes to rutilated quartz and is excellent for banishing depression, fears or anxieties. The "anti-stress" crystal, this form of quartz will also alleviate physical stress and applying it to an area of pain will help to reduce the pain.

- Milky or snow; a gentle crystal that aids with meditation and promotes wisdom. This is a good meditation crystal which will help you to achieve a deep level of concentration and connection to your inner self. Like clear quartz it can be used as a general healing crystal but is gentler and slower to act.

Tiger's Eye

Another crystal that comes in a variety of colors, these beautiful and iridescent stones are flecked with luxuriant color. Tiger's eye has long been associated as a talisman stone, that protects and brings good luck. In general, the stone will bring feelings of self-worth and confidence. It both grounds and creates a sense of connection with the higher, spiritual world. Tiger's eye will, in general, bring good luck and is particularly associated with removing blockages in life.

- Blue; often a very dark bluish-green, this crystal brings enlightenment and confidence. This protective stone is used to find your true abilities and talents. In healing it is a good stone to help with cognitive disorders or for those who find it difficult to express themselves.
- Red; as with other red stones this crystal is linked with protection and also combat. This provides both self-

knowledge and confidence; it's a stone that will help to banish fears or doubts and help the user to forge ahead in life. In healing it can be helped to overcome sexual difficulties and is also good for healing fatigue related illnesses.

Topaz

This popular gem is also an excellent crystal for use in healing. The delicate blue of topaz is linked to bright, clear skies and therefore to mental prowess and clarity of thought. It heals the spirit, creates openness to both others and to new concepts. It also promotes honesty, integrity and trust. Topaz can help to heal mental problems, anxiety and is a powerful stone for creating a deep link to the spiritual. Many healers choose this stone as their own, personal talisman to bring them strength and clarity in their work.

Turquoise

Like jade, this crystal has long been prized for its decorative and healing qualities. It is used to protect against negative influences from others and is also strongly associated with fresh, invigorating air. This makes it a useful stone in healing for dealing with breathing related disorders and lung problems. It can also have a deeply calming affect, making it useful for dealing with many issues including public speaking or to boost confidence in any venture. The clear, fresh nature of the gem sweeps away self-doubt and negative moods.

Conclusion

Thank you again for getting this book!

I hope this book was able to help you understand the uses of crystals for healing.

The next step is to find the crystals that are right for you and use them to benefit your life and heal.

Finally, if you enjoyed this book, please take the time to share your thoughts and post a review on Amazon. It'd be greatly appreciated!

Thank you and good luck!

CPSIA information can be obtained
at www.ICGtesting.com
Printed in the USA
LVHW080506271222
735859LV00006B/502

9 781989 785195